Microgreens

*How to Grow Organic Superfood Indoors
and Create Your Own Profitable Business*

Contents

Introduction

Have you ever had the pleasure of eating fruit straight from the tree or eating a salad that has been made with homegrown vegetables? Or have you ever had seafood that has been freshly caught and cooked? If you haven't, you are definitely missing out, and if you have, you know just how amazing it can be. What if you could enjoy that fresh-tasting scrumptiousness and even profit from your surplus production?

Getting involved in growing your own food, whether vegetables, fruit, or microgreens, is always exciting. If you can channel that into being a side hustle or even a full-time income, this would be the cream of the crop. Creating side gigs and passive sources of income is all the rage right now, and what could be more passive than a plant that just requires you to give it the nutrients it needs and does everything else on its own.

Growing microgreens is a fun experience, and because most people aren't very familiar with the basics of growing anything, they think it is a complicated procedure that requires a lot of knowledge, skills, and money. If you want to take your microgreen farming to a commercial scale, then it will require a combination of all those resources. However, little do people know it can be done quite inexpensively from the comfort of their own home. At most, all that's required is a few feet of space, and you need to be consistent with maintenance in the initial phase.

Throughout this book, you'll learn everything you need to know to put together a fantastic microgreen farm at home that will yield enough for you to eat and a surplus that you can sell.

If you are worried about the selling part, we have got you covered in that area, too. You will learn about everything you need to know to kick start a small microgreen business – from finding customers and putting together a marketing plan right through to selling the products and making your first profit. We have all the information you need. More importantly, this book has advice from the best specialists in the field of microgreen farming and microgreen selling so you can be sure that you are getting it from the horse's mouth.

More significantly, we have mapped out the entire life cycle of microgreens together with a similar life cycle for your business, so you have something to refer to at every stage of your journey.

We have put the information and resources together in this book so that someone who has never been in business or even watered a plant in their lives can develop their green thumb and start growing after reading this book and using no additional resources. This is not just theoretical knowledge about plants. It is practical everyday information that you can put to use right after every chapter. With a minimal investment of both time and money, we can help you delve into this incredibly rewarding hobby and even start making good money. If that sounds like something you would be interested in, let's get started!

Chapter 1: Microgreens and Business

Microgreens were first introduced to the Californian restaurant scene in the 1980s, but now, they're reputable in the fine dining arena all around the globe. You may hear them being called vegetable confetti, micro herbs, or little greens – and regardless of what they're called, they've steadily gained popularity over the years. If it's your first time hearing of the term, you're probably more familiar with microgreens as the fancy aromatic greens that are splashed over micro-servings in fancy restaurants. Since most of us enjoy a healthy and somewhat large appetite, the idea of eating a micro-serving may be enough to steer you away from microgreens – but this is where you'll be missing out.

Just because fancy restaurants use them doesn't mean you have to follow their lead in regard to the portion size. In fact, shouldn't you wonder why these fancy dishes are so popular, despite being so little? You'll definitely understand the appeal once you try adding some microgreen to your dishes. The rich aroma, the unique taste, and the nutritional punch that comes with adding microgreens to your diet are simply unparalleled. Once you get your hands on these greens, you'll never be able to go back to your old ways of making food!

Let's take a deeper look into microgreens to understand why they're highly sought-after and why you should definitely add them to your diet. Once we've covered that, we'll delve deeper into why starting a microgreen business can be one of the best ventures you can explore.

What Are Microgreens?

Microgreens are akin to the teenage version of sprouts. They're young, green vegetables that grow to be around 1 to 3 inches, or 2. 5 to 7.5 cm, in height. The height of the plant depends on the nature of the seed and how fast it grows, but one thing is sure – all kinds of microgreens are super delicate to the touch.

They have a strong aromatic flavor, can have a variety of colors and textures, and generally pack a lot of nutritional value. You can grow microgreens from any vegetable or herb, in soil or hydroponically, indoors or in greenhouses, and, as long as you can give them sunlight, you can choose your planting setting.

The term "microgreens" isn't limited to one kind or family of plants. Rather, it's the baby version of a plant harvested somewhere after it becomes a sprout and before it becomes a baby green. When they were first discovered in the '80s, they were limited to 5 varieties of plants, but now, we've progressed into growing more than 25 varieties. You may already be familiar with a few microgreens if you're using parsley, fennel, cilantro, basil, beets, or cabbage in your cooking.

That said, microgreens are not sprouts. Sprouts generally do not have leaves, but microgreens do. Sprouts also grow much faster, taking a cycle of 2 to 7 days to flourish. Meanwhile, microgreens take anywhere from 1 to 3 weeks to be harvested, right after they show their first true leaves.

Microgreens are not baby greens either, though they're similar in that both their leaves and stems are edible. However, microgreens are much smaller than baby greens. They can also be sold before harvest as a whole plant to be kept alive at home until it's time to eat them.

Why Are Microgreens So Popular?

There are many reasons why microgreens are so popular nowadays. As our awareness of global trends increases, we become more educated about various scientific facts. That's why we've grown to love microgreens more than other vegetables since we know they hold the following properties:

Microgreens Are Superfoods

Have you heard of the term "superfoods" before? It's used to describe food that's packed with nutrition. This is one of the major reasons microgreens are popular, and, oh boy, do they have a powerful nutritional punch! You wouldn't believe something so miniature could add such great value to your diet. To give you some perspective, eating a 100 gm serving of basil and sunflower microgreen mixture is worth 28 calories. However, with these 28 calories, you'll get:

- 4.4 grams of carbohydrate
- 2.2 grams of protein
- 2.2 grams of fiber
- 11 mg of sodium
- 66 mg of magnesium
- 15.9 mg of iron
- 88 milligrams of calcium
- 298 milligrams of potassium
- 0.7 milligrams of zinc
- 66 milligrams of phosphorus
- 66 micrograms of folate
- 79.6 micrograms of vitamin A
- 6.6 milligrams of vitamin C
- In addition to B vitamins, manganese, and selenium.

That's something you can try so hard to get with other vegetables and fruit, even less so by ingesting a mixture of only two varieties. The nutritional value you get will change depending on the microgreens you use, but you can rest assured that you'll satisfy your micro and macro nutritional needs by adding microgreens to your diet.

As you can see, the greatest thing about microgreens is that their nutritional value is concentrated. Although they're smaller than baby greens, the way they're grown condenses the nutritional value to make them more valuable. The microgreen version of a baby green can contain anywhere from 4 to 40 times the nutritional value of a particular nutrient. So, imagine how valuable it'd be to grow a superfood in the form of microgreens – it's like you're creating a super-superfood.

1. They Have Intense Flavors and Great Visual Appeal

Their condensed nutritional value does more than provide value to your meals. It also serves in condensing their colors. Due to this, you'd be hard-pressed to find a food garnish or dressing that appeases the eye as much as adding microgreens to your plates. Microgreens are strongly aromatic, giving them unique tastes and intense flavors. You can take your pick of the microgreens you want to savor, choosing between crisp, tangy, earthy, mellow, or nutty textures. Whichever kind you choose, you'll be sure to savor every bite and enjoy your food more. To make it even better, microgreens have a unique textural contrast that varies from their fully grown-plant counterparts.

2. They're Easy to Grow

There are only two caveats to keep in mind when you decide to try microgreens. You'll probably be shocked at how pricey they are, but even if you overlook that, you may not be able to find them readily available in your local stores. Luckily for all of us, growing microgreens is so easy. It's so easy that you'll think there must be another catch – but there isn't. It will take one to three weeks to have the microgreens at your fingertips. You can grow them outdoors, in a greenhouse, or on your windowsill. You can take your pick from various seeds of herbs or vegetables. Just provide them with sunlight and the environment they need, and you can plant your microgreens any time of the year – or even all year round!

3. They're Sustainable

Thanks to their low-growing needs, microgreens are a great solution for sustainable food. They can be grown locally, even in limited or confined spaces, while giving you bulky and variable harvests that can satisfy the local community's needs. Since they have a short cycle of 1 to 3 weeks, they can satisfy local demand all year long. Microgreens are even being studied as a nutritional option to provide great food for astronauts in space. How cool is that? They're literally out of this world!

Health Benefits of Microgreens

Now you can understand why microgreens are so popular, but everything we've discussed so far can be considered public knowledge. If you really want to appreciate the superfoods that make up microgreens, it's worth looking into their myriad health benefits. It turns out these superfoods can do wonders for your physical and mental health. Here's a quick overview of just how beneficial microgreens are:

1. They're Rich in Antioxidant Content

Most plants and vegetables are already rich in antioxidants, which makes the content of antioxidants in microgreens even higher. Antioxidants are unparalleled when it comes to getting rid of free radicals – harmful waste molecules that accumulate inside the human body.

Naturally, the body has its own mechanisms to remove these free radicals, but there are times when the free radicals exceed the body's ability to deal with them. Free radicals can be created either as a natural side effect of internal body functions or due to external pressure, such as being exposed to pollution. When these free radicals build up inside the body, they start destroying cells. The cellular damage resulting from free radicals has been associated with various conditions and diseases, like accelerated aging, cancer, and other chronic conditions.

With that in mind, the high antioxidant content in microgreens helps the body to regain control and fight the free radicals, which, in turn, maintains a healthy internal balance. The content and antioxidants differ according to which kind of microgreens are eaten. For instance, microgreens from the Asteraceae family, such as lettuce, contain high levels of carotenoid antioxidants – otherwise known as vitamin A. Meanwhile, Brassica microgreens, like broccoli, have high phenolic antioxidant amounts, otherwise known as vitamin E.

2. They Reduce the Risk of Various Diseases

Although scientists are optimistic, using microgreens to treat specific diseases is still being researched. That said, the exceptional amount of vitamins, minerals, and antioxidants present in microgreens make them greatly beneficial for an individual's general health. Although they're still being studied, it's safe to assume they can provide the same health benefits as eating green vegetables – if not more health benefits. Nevertheless, eating greens and vegetables has been proven to decrease the risk factor for the following diseases and conditions:

• **Heart Disease:** The antioxidants in microgreens lower the risk of heart disease, especially due to their ability to lower LDL – or bad cholesterol – from the bloodstream.

• **Diabetes:** Surprisingly, microgreens can have a calming effect on the body, lowering the amount of stress a person experiences. This kind of stress can interfere with the body's ability to transport sugar into the cells, creating diabetes.

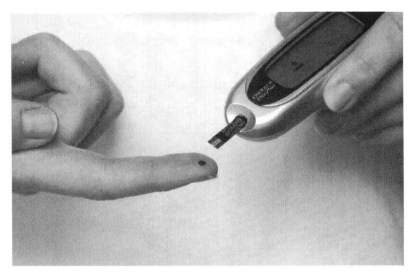

• **Certain Cancers:** Once again, it's the antioxidant effect. Antioxidants present in microgreens, or any other healthy food, help the body combat free radicals, which have been significantly linked to different kinds of cancers.

All things considered, it's important to note that further studies need to be done to confirm the health benefits of microgreens when it comes to specific diseases.

3. They Can Be Tailored to Groups of Specific Needs

Certain groups require special nutritional needs due to the demanding nature of their specific ailments or lifestyles. This includes people with serious chronic diseases, like those living with kidney disease or people following certain diets, like vegans, vegetarians, or raw-food dieters. While it can be hard to find suitable alternatives for meat, carbs, and other nutrients, there's nothing easier than fulfilling the nutritional demands by adding microgreens, the ultimate superfood, into your diet.

4. They Provide Additional Health Benefits

Microgreens can offer a myriad of health benefits, depending on the kind you're eating. They may help boost your immune system, improve your eyesight, improve bowel movements and regularity, and reduce constipation. They also help to maintain a healthy digestive system. They also play a role in maintaining one's psychological and mental health.

Are There Any Risks to Eating Supergreens?

Microgreens are generally safe for ingestion. You shouldn't worry about eating them any more than you would any other greens. However, there is a catch – whether it comes to greens or microgreens, ascertaining the purity of the food is essential. Microgreens can cause food poisoning if grown in unsanitary conditions or if bacteria or other microorganisms infect them. The potential for growing bacteria and microorganisms is much lower in microgreens than in other baby greens and sprouts.

We cover potential risks further on in this book, but if you're planning to grow your microgreens at home, you need to be sure of the quality of the seeds you're using. Always look for a reputable company to get your seeds from, and make sure the medium you're using is free from contaminants and harmful microorganisms, like E. coli and Salmonella.

How to Eat Microgreens

You can add microgreens to your diet in a variety of ways. You'll only be limited by your imagination! Invariably, microgreens are a great addition to a plethora of dishes. Since they're basically greens, you can vary your dishes by adding them to Keto, Mediterranean, Atkin's, gluten-free, vegan, vegetarian, DASH, and practically any kind of diet you're following. If you're unsure of where to start, here are a few ideas about how you can add microgreens to your diet.

1. Add Microgreens to Your Salad

You can never go wrong if you decide to eat microgreens raw. Simply note a few key points. For a start, keeping them away from heat is the best way to preserve their nutritional value, which is bound to decrease during any form of cooking. Moreover, leaving them fresh will allow you to enjoy their crisp and delicate flavors as nature intended it to be. You can eat them on their own or add them to your salads – Greek, tuna, Cesar, green mix, or any kind of salad that tickles your fancy.

2. Spice up Your Cooking with Microgreens

You may have to experiment a bit before becoming confident about it, but how about you have some fun using microgreens as spices? You can try adding them to your soups, stir fry dishes – or even fresh-veggie pasta. Alternatively, you can try adding them to omelets, pizzas, curry, or other savory dishes.

3. Make Nutritious Juices and Smoothies with Microgreens

Do you like juices? Do you often run out of ideas for your post-workout smoothie? If that's the case, it's time to rev up your drinking game by introducing microgreens.

4. Try Adding Microgreens to Your Baking

It may sound weird at first but think about it. You already make spinach souffle or quiche with spinach; why not add sunflower microgreens instead? What about adding a taste of radish to your summer berry pie? There's no wrong way to bake your microgreens. You can opt for whichever way works for you.

Reasons to Start Your Microgreen Business

You can certainly try growing microgreens for fun, but what about growing them from a business perspective? There are a few reasons why starting a microgreen business may be the best venture of your life. Here's a sneak peek:

1. Microgreen Demand Is Increasing at a Terrifying Pace

The use of microgreens in making various dishes is expanding now more than ever. Its use is not limited to fancy restaurants anymore – practically every kind of cuisine is now experimenting by adding microgreens to their menus. You'll also find it more common now to come across packed microgreens in local grocery stores, frozen or powdered microgreens in health and supplement stores, or in the fridge of home chefs. The moral of the story is that you'll find high demand on your microgreen business, wherever you decide to set up and regardless of your target customer segment.

2. Microgreens Have a Fast Turnaround Time

Unlike other vegetables and fruit, the turnaround period for growing microgreens is extremely short. You may be ready to pack the first cycle of the microgreen batch in as short as one week, and the most it will take you is three weeks. As previously mentioned, it all depends on the kind of microgreens you're planning to grow. Other factors can affect the turnaround time, like how you want to deliver them. We'll also go into more detail about that in a later chapter.

3. You Can Use Microgreens to Add Value to Your Current Business

If you're already in the business of growing plants, adding microgreens to your list can be a valuable addition. You've already got the environment and supplements all set up, so adding a new crop will cost you very little. Moreover, you have your target customers defined, and you know where your demand comes from. Convincing your current customers to try one more superfood product will be practically seamless.

4. The Cost of Starting up Is Low

Starting up a microgreen business is great in many ways, one of which is that it only requires a surprisingly low budget to get started. Thanks to the variety of growing options available, you can plant them outdoors if you already have fertile soil, indoors in some racks and trays, or use a hydroponic system to grow them without any soil at all.

5. Provide Enormous Value to Your Customers

We've already established the nutritional value of microgreens. The good thing is that people have become much more aware of their nutritional needs, and they're willing to pay a good price to get their hands on these superfoods. The legwork is pretty much done for you – you won't even need to convince any customers to buy your products.

6. You Can Grow Microgreens All Year Round

Unlike other plants that require specific growing conditions, microgreens have simple needs. You'll be able to grow your plants all year round without worrying about the downtime needed to turn the soil or wait for the right season. Add the short turnaround time to that, and you'll be raking in profits in no time.

7. You'll Get High Return on Investment

Perhaps the most important factor in any business is profit, and a microgreen business *won't disappoint.* Most startup costs go into setting up the business, but you won't need a hefty initial investment to get started. Granted, you'll need to invest a bit in the supplies and packaging, but that will soon be covered once you sell the first few batches.

Regardless of how you look at it, microgreens are a miracle discovery. The plants pack a nutritional punch that's hard to match with any other kind of food. That gives them a great advantage regarding health benefits and cuisine additions. Best of all, you can easily plant your own microgreens to reap their benefits, or you can take it one step further and start a profitable microgreen business.

Chapter 2: The Bare Necessities

When planning to start any business, one needs to be ready to dedicate a certain amount of time to getting started. You'll need to provide a space, set a budget, and acquire resources to get things going. In this aspect, growing microgreens for profit is no different – you'll need to approach it with a business mindset to succeed. So, what exactly does this "business mindset" mean? And just how much time, effort, and resources should you dedicate to this venture? If this is sending you into a state of panic, don't fret! By the end of this chapter, you'll be equipped with all you need to be well on your way to starting a most successful microgreen business.

Now, let's get started with the bare necessities.

Just How Profitable Is a Microgreen Business?

Let's just get one thing out of the way first so you can focus on the primary aspects of starting the microgreen business. You must be curious about how profitable your microgreen venture can be.

There are a lot of factors that can affect your profit. For starters, the scale on which you'll start to grow will make the biggest difference. Starting by growing eight trays of a microgreen variety will yield less profit than growing 50 trays, but it's more common to start small and experiment with the process rather than go all out and risk losing your investment due to failure. Therefore, it's best to expect a small profit at first until you learn the ropes and develop your own growth process, after which you can scale up to the desired degree. There are also a lot of other internal and external factors that can affect your profit, but we'll get to that later.

The profit you get can be calculated based on two aspects: the costs you'll incur and the gross profit you'll make from selling. By subtracting the cost from gross profit, you'll be able to calculate the net profit, which is a true estimate of what you'll be earning. Let's take a case study to get the numbers in perspective.

The main factor determining your profit is the number of trays you'll sell. On average, one tray will carry around 10 to 15 ounces (oz) of microgreen yield, while the price of one ounce will range between $1.25 and $2. You may be able to cash in $2 per ounce if you're able to sell them quickly, but the older they get, the lower the price. They also have a shelf life of 2 to 3 days, after which they'll start to wilt and die. This means if you sell one tray of 10 ounces of microgreens, you can earn $10.25 to $20. So, if you start with ten trays per week and repeat the process three times per month, and assuming you sell each tray for $20, you could make a $600 gross profit per month.

You'll have to subtract the cost you incurred during the process. A ballpark estimate of the costs Of growing ten trays three times per month can go as follows:

- $20 for the trays
- $40 for the lights
- $150 for the seeds
- $60 for the growing mats
- And $15 for the packaging of 30 boxes

This adds up to $295 as the total cost for the month. Bearing this in mind, the net profit is $600-$295=$305. You can expect this number to increase since some of the equipment costs will be fixed costs which you'll only pay once.

What Are the Total Costs of Running a Microgreen Business?

There's something you should be aware of when calculating the costs. We've mentioned it briefly, but you'll incur two kinds of costs which are fixed and variable.

Fixed costs refer to the kind of costs you'll pay only once – it's the initial payment you'll make for the items you'll keep using for growing a lot of trays, in contrast to the additional costs you'll incur for each tray. Those kinds of costs are known as *variable costs*. So, while you'll calculate the fixed costs only once, you'll multiply the variable costs according to the number of items you'll need to use periodically. Let's take a look at another example to clarify.

In the list of fixed costs, you'll add the following:

- Trays at an average price of $2 per tray.
- Lighting will cost you around $50 for growing ten trays.

As for the variable costs, you'll incur the following:

- Seeds at an average of $5 per ounce, although the price of different microgreen varieties will certainly be different.
- Growing mats (in case you decide to grow your plants without soil), which will be at an average of $2 per mat, and you'll need one mat per tray.
- Packaging boxes, which can be around 50 cents for one box, which makes $5 for the total packaging of 10 trays.

You may incur additional costs if you decide to get more supplies and equipment, which you most probably will. We'll discuss the full list of the necessary equipment further down in this chapter, but these are the major costs you'll incur throughout the time you run your microgreen business.

How Much Time Will You Have to Dedicate to Your Business?

Now that you can rest assured about the income, let's discuss the other factors you'll need to consider for your microgreens business. The first factor will be time, which can be tricky if you start a side hustle alongside your main job or business. However, how much time you need to dedicate will depend purely on the business scale you have in mind.

If you want to start small with a dozen trays per week in a limited space, you can consider a part-time job that only requires 15 to 30 minutes of your time per day. This amount of time will increase slightly during harvesting and selling. However, if you're running a huge-scale business that you hope to earn more than six figures from, you can expect to need to treat it as a full-time job. You'll need a few sets of additional hands to help you with the process of growing, harvesting, and selling, so you'll need to hire a couple of employees as well.

In short, your microgreen business can take up as much or as little of your time as you choose. That's one of the greatest advantages of this type of business. After all, you can scale it up or down as you choose and as is fitting for your circumstances.

How Much Space Do You Need to Start Growing Microgreens?

Here's another flexible aspect of growing microgreens. You can start with the least amount of space or dedicate a whole field to it. You don't need a lot of space to start, and you can practically start using a spare bedroom! In fact, it's a well-known strategy among microgreen cultivators to use their empty vertical space to the maximum capacity. Since you'll be growing your harvest in racks, you can install shelves along your walls to create your racks. A 60 square foot space can hold racks of four shelves and give rise to 50 pounds of microgreens cultivated throughout a 2-week cycle. If you sold each pound for $20, you could make $1000 every two weeks – or $2000 per month!

However, you can also take a simpler route, start with a tabletop, and grow a few trays until you get the hang of the process. Once you decide to grow microgreens on a professional level, you'll want to rent a bigger space to scale up your business.

The Necessary Equipment Needed to Start Your Own Microgreen Business

Now, let's look into all the items and equipment pieces you'll need when growing microgreens. Here's a list of both the essential tools and accessories you may find useful throughout your processes:

1. Shelving Racks

The first thing you'll need is shelving racks to place your trays. You may settle for a tabletop at first, but if you're planning on growing microgreens as a business venture, you'll need a larger space. In this aspect, installing shelving racks is the best way to optimize your space without renting extra rooms. You can simply buy a classic storage rack and turn it into your working space or build something by hand if you're into DIY projects. Any material will suffice as long as it's functional and can do the job.

2. Trays and Containers

You'll need something to plant your seeds on, and trays provide a wonderful way. However, you can use any kind of container as long as it has drain holes to keep the excess water running off. The tray's dimensions will help you calculate your yield and estimate your profits, so you can start with 10"x 20" trays and get the number according to your desired harvest amount. You can also get normal trays and drill the holes yourself – there's no right or wrong to choosing trays; just use the best option for you.

3. Lights

Lights are an essential item for growing microgreens, especially if you'll be growing microgreens indoors. The artificial lights should provide enough light for the seeds to grow strong, straight, and tall. You can start with a 2-bulb, 4-foot fluorescent fixture that you'll install over each rack and install basic T8 fluorescent bulbs on the fixtures.

4. The Growing Medium

There are a lot of options for growing microgreens. You may choose high-quality potting soil, preferably organic, but you can forgo the soil altogether and choose other growing mediums. A few of these mediums include coco peat, coco mats, hemp mats, Rockwool, and bamboo mats.

5. The Seeds

The quality of the seeds you get can make or break your yield. It's best to get quality seeds from a reputable vendor and even better if you get organic seeds. Choose seeds that are easy to grow and experiment first with a small batch before going all out. That way, you can limit your losses in case of a faulty batch.

6. A Spray Bottle

Especially during the germination phase, you'll need to keep your seeds well-hydrated and cared for. The best way is to thoroughly (and regularly) mist the seeds you've sown using a spray bottle. It's also better to choose a spray bottle with an adjustable end so you can adjust it depending on the microgreen variety you're misting.

7. Airflow and Ventilation

Like all plants, microgreens need and love fresh air. Merely opening your windows and doors can create a decent airflow at first, but you'll need to set up an airflow system if you're running a wide-scale business. Maintaining good airflow and installing a dehumidifier can help keep your plants well-ventilated and dry, which will protect them against mold and other issues.

8. Additional Accessories

In addition to the previous items, you may want to speed up and grow your business with the following accessories:

•Paper towels to cover the seeds for germination.

•A measuring scale to weigh your microgreens. A small scale to measure the seeds before planting them and a larger one to measure the trays before packaging them.

•You'll need a timer to schedule your lights to turn on and off at the designated times.

•You'll make good use of a small fan to help you ventilate the crops and prevent mold development or other issues.

•A pair of scissors and/or sharp knives to help you harvest. Remember that a sharp blade will make the process a breeze, while dull blades can make harvesting a dreadful task.

•A watering can. Once your microgreens grow larger, you'll prefer to switch to watering them instead of misting them with water through the spray bottle.

•3% hydrogen peroxide to create the spraying solution. Adding hydrogen peroxide to the solution is a great way to prevent the development of molds.

•Measuring spoons to add your seeds to the tray and measure an accurate amount,

•A "pusher" for the soil – something you can make. This tool aims to help you prepare the soil evenly, which will help you during the process of sowing the seeds.

•If you don't have a workbench at home, you'll need a table to start your operation.

•Something for packaging. Plastic clamshells are the most popular choice. You may want to invest in something more sustainable, like cellulose composting packaging.

•Labels to identify your packaged crops and list their details. Be sure to choose labels of the right size, as you don't want to miss out on adding key details onto labels that are too small. You'll need to add your logo, company name, crop weight, date of packaging, and other crop details.

•You'll also need bins to store your dry soil and dispose of what's left after you harvest your trays. It's safe to say that two large bins will suffice, but it all comes down to the scale of your operation.

•You'll need a climate gauge to monitor your room temperature and humidity. This will help you know if the airflow and ventilation are running smoothly and efficiently.

•Suppose you are running marketing operations for your business. In that case, you'll probably need a printer to print your labels, pricing list, and business invoices.

•Consider getting a date stamp to add the date details of the harvest before you sell them, as most retail outlets will ask you to add the "harvested on" or "best before" date on the label.

All in all, your supplies should cost you a few hundred dollars at first. The cost you'll incur depends on the scale of your operation. Once you get used to running smooth and efficient operations, you'll be able to reinvest your profits to scale up your operations and then break even once again with the increased profit.

General Tips to Start Your Microgreen Business

Starting a business is no small feat, even if it sounds as easy as starting a microgreen business. There are a lot of factors you need to consider before you begin. Otherwise, you may be backed into a corner – thanks to uninformed decisions. On that note, here are some crucial factors to keep in mind before starting your microgreen business.

1. Your Location Makes All the Difference in the World

Although there's a high demand for microgreens worldwide, that doesn't mean that they'll sell anywhere. You'll need to choose a good location where the local community understands the importance of microgreens. As to the location for *growing your microgreens,* find a suitable environment so that you won't struggle with getting the seeds, growing medium, or getting the necessary supplies for your microgreens. You can order many things online, but then there's the wait time for shipping; better to locate stores nearby when possible.

2. You'll Need to Dedicate Time

Although you can start a microgreen business without consuming a lot of time, you must still dedicate a good amount of your time to the venture. The process may not take a lot of time, and you may be able to find ways to make things time-efficient, but there's more to starting a business than running operations. Before you get started, you'll need to research the market and devise your business plan. Throughout the whole process of running a business, you'll need to invest time and resources in marketing and reaching out to potential customers. Once you've grown your batches, you'll need to harvest them, package, and sell your products. All of these tasks will require a good amount of time and focus.

3. Bring Your Passion to the Table

There's more to starting a business than simply earning a profit, although that certainly plays a big role. However, if you're about to invest your time, effort, and resources into something, you might as well bring your passion to the table. You'll quickly experience burnout if you're not enjoying what you're doing, and you may become careless with your operation's efficiency.

4. Start Small

Don't feel pressured to make money, and don't let the appeal of how profitable a microgreen business can get the better of you. After careful planning, take the necessary actions but *start small*. Be patient; no one expects you to have customers right away. It's best to start your business as a hobby and slowly work your way up from there.

5. Keep It Simple

There are dozens of microgreen varieties you can start with, but just because you *can*, doesn't mean you *should*. Start with simple microgreens and learn the process correctly, and then you can try adding a new variety. You should certainly enjoy the growing process, but you should also ensure that there is a market demand for your products.

6. Focus On the Efficiency of Your Procedures

Instead of diverting your attention toward a thousand different tasks or a dozen microgreen varieties, it may be better to stick to a couple of plants initially and learn everything there is to learn about them. That way, you'll become aware of needless or redundant tasks that take up your time. With a bit of trial and error, you'll be able to carry out the most efficient process of growing, harvesting, packaging, and selling – making your next scale-up much easier.

7. Learn from the Best, and Keep Learning

Finally, keep in mind that learning is a lifelong process. However, everyone starts from zero. There's also a fortune of knowledge and experience waiting for you from people who've walked this path before you, so be sure to follow their advice and learn from their mistakes. You don't need to reinvent the wheel. You just need to figure out how to improve it.

Although starting a microgreen business is a promising and profitable venture, you can't just dive into it without adequate preparation. First of all, you'll need to study the list of necessary supplies and determine how to get quality products. You'll also need to analyze the other demands of the business, whether this means time, location, resources, or general knowledge. Once you're confident you've done your homework, you can then embark.

Chapter 3: Types of Microgreens

We have discussed in previous chapters what microgreens are, their benefits, and how to start a microgreens business. In this chapter, we will discuss the different types of seedlings and how they grow. There are many types of microgreens out there, and these are usually categorized by *family*.

Microgreen Families

- **The Lamiaceae Family**

This family includes some of the most popular and most commonly used herbs, such as sage, mint, rosemary, oregano, cilantro, and basil.

- **The Apiaceae Family**

This family includes herbs and vegetables such as dill, carrots, fennel, and celery.

- **The Poaceae Family**

You'll find in this family various cereals and grasses such as rice, barley, oats, wheatgrass, and oats. This family also includes legumes such as lentils, beans, and chickpeas.

- **The Amaranthaceae Family**

The members of this family include spinach, beets, chard, quinoa, and amaranth.

- **The Asteraceae Family**

You'll find lettuce, chicory, radicchio, and endive in this family.

- **The Cucurbitaceae Family**

This family includes fruit such as pumpkins, melons, squashes, and cucumbers.

- **The Amaryllidaceae Family**

Some of the most popular vegetables are in this family, such as onions, garlic, leeks, and chives.

- **The Brassicaceae Family**

Some of the most colorful vegetables are a part of this family, like cauliflower, radish, cabbage, watercress, broccoli, and arugula.

Now that you have familiarized yourself with the different families of microgreens, let's take a look at the types of microgreens and how to grow them.

Types of Microgreens and How They Grow

Radishes

If you are a beginner and are looking for something simple to grow, we suggest starting with radishes. They are extremely popular, delicious, and look beautiful. It is very easy to grow this vegetable, and it only takes about 5 to 10 days to harvest them. It isn't necessary to pre-soak the seeds. However, if you want your seeds to grow faster, you can pre-soak them for about 4 to 6 hours.

You'll need a growing tray with drainage holes. Fill it with moist soil, and smooth the surface. Spread the seeds evenly and then mist them with a water spray. You'll need to cover the growing tray with another one since radishes require darkness to grow.

After 2 to 3 days, the radishes will start to sprout so you can remove the second tray. At this stage, radishes will need 12 hours of light every day. After a few days, you'll notice your radish growing into red or white stems. You'll need to bottom water the soil every couple of days. Fill a watering dish and put the tray into it to achieve this. Leave it for about 15 to 20 minutes, and make sure that the soil soaks up enough water before removing the tray.

Radish microgreens will flourish best in soil or hydroponically. The soil must be rich in organic matter. If it isn't, add all-purpose fertilizer or old compost to the soil. Start harvesting the radish when the plant is 2 to 3 inches tall. It isn't recommended to leave them in the ground for a long time after they have grown.

Radishes have many health benefits since they contain vitamin C and various antioxidants; they have a mild spicy flavor. This vegetable is used in many recipes and can also be the perfect addition to a salad or sandwich.

Pea Shoots

Another microgreen that is easy to grow is the pea shoot. This delicious, crunchy vegetable has many health benefits since it contains vitamins A, C, E, B1, B2, and B3 and minerals, proteins, and fiber.

You'll need to pre-soak the seeds for about 12 to 24 hours before you plant them. The seeds must absorb a lot of water, so make sure to fill the bowl to the top. The pea shoot seeds are usually huge, which means that they will take up more space. Therefore, you'll need to use more of them if you hope to have a thicker harvest. Plant the seeds in a thick layer. You'll need three trays, and only one must have drainage holes. The other two will be used for germination and watering. You'll fill the one with drainage holes with soil and seeds. Ensure the soil is smooth, then spread the seeds evenly. You'll need to cover the seeds with a thin layer of soil. Cover the tray and leave it for 3 to 4 days. By then, the seeds should have grown into long pea sprouts.

Since these seedlings require a lot of water, make sure that you bottom water the soil two to three times a day. You need your soil to be moist rather than soggy, or the plants may rot. It is recommended to use artificial light rather than sunlight since it is more effective. Pea sprouts are usually ready for harvest when they grow 3 to 4 inches tall, which takes about 8 to 12 days. The best growth medium for this vegetable is soil or hydroponics.

Beetroots

Beetroots, or as they are commonly known beets, are very popular vegetables with many health benefits. One of the reasons they are so favored is that they come in beautiful colors; red hues, pink, and green. Like radishes, beets are very easy to grow, making them the perfect plants to start with if you are a first timer. They usually take a longer time to grow compared to other microgreens, but this delicious vegetable is worth the wait. Beets have a sweet and earthy flavor, making them a great addition to any meal you make. They have many nutritional benefits since they contain many vitamins like A, B, C, E, and K. They also contain protein, iron, zinc, calcium, potassium, and magnesium.

Before you plant the seeds, they need to be soaked for about 10 to 12 hours in cold water. Pre-soaking the seeds will improve their germination rate. The trays you are using must have proper drainage because beets don't require a lot of water. Fill the tray with soil, dampen the soil using a misting bottle, and then smooth the soil out. Spread the seeds evenly onto the surface, mist it one last time with water, and cover it with another tray. Leave them for four to six days. By then, the seeds should be growing, so you'll need to remove the tray and expose them to light. You'll have to bottom water the soil whenever it is dry.

Blackout time for beets is about five to six days, germination time is about two to three days, and harvest is after about 8 to 12 days. Once the leaves open and the plants start showing the beautiful colors we mentioned earlier, it is time to harvest.

Cress

Cress is another microgreen that is very easy to grow. It has a tangy, spicy flavor and is very delicious. Cress is rich in vitamins like B, C, and K. It also contains iron and fiber. Unlike the other seeds mentioned here, cress seeds don't require pre-soaking. This is mainly because the seed is gel coated, meaning that it needs less water during its sprouting period. Although the other microgreen seeds mentioned in this chapter need water to increase the germination rate, wet cress seeds can lead to a lower germination rate. Lightly spray the seeds and ensure the soil isn't too moist.

To plant your seeds, you'll need to dampen the top surface of the grow tray. When sowing the seeds, you need them to *stick,* staying where you put them instead of blowing off or sticking together. Next, you should spread the seeds evenly over the tray. Afterward, mist the seeds lightly, unlike you usually do with other seeds, and cover them. After 3 to 4 days, your seeds will start sprouting. Once they appear, they will require light. Keep watering the seeds but don't overdo it. The seeds should be damp rather than wet. The soil should be moist because cress needs a low water environment to grow and flourish. Cress is ready to harvest when it is between 1 ½ and 2 inches high.

Sunflower

The sunflower can be a great addition to any salad and is a snack favored by people of all ages due to its sweet, nutty, and crunchy flavor. This is probably why this microgreen is very popular. Sunflower microgreens have many nutritional benefits since they contain iron, proteins, calcium, amino acids, potassium, magnesium, and vitamins A, B, C, D, and K. They are also easily digested. You can either grow sunflower seeds in soil or with a hydroponic medium. The sunflower seeds need to be pre-soaked for about 24 hours to soften their shell and increase germination. Once the seeds start sprouting, you can place them in a growing tray with drainage holes. However, before taking this step, you'll need to put some water in the tray then place the soil on top. Fill the tray with soil, then smooth it over. Make sure you spread the seeds evenly to cover the soil's surface. Be careful not to overlap the seeds.

Mist the seeds and cover them with another tray. Mist them twice a day while keeping the cover on. They will start sprouting after a few days, but expect them to appear discolored because they have yet to be exposed to light. You should then remove the cover and expose them to grow lights for about 12 to 18 hours every day. Keep them very close to the light. When the plant is 3 to 4 inches high, then this means that they are ready to harvest. To avoid the flavor turning bitter, harvest before the leaves start growing. The harvest time is usually between 8 and 12 days.

Broccoli

Broccoli is another type of microgreen that beginners can easily grow, and they grow very quickly. This microgreen is rich in vitamins A, C, K, protein, and calcium. Broccoli doesn't need much water, so you won't have to pre-soak the seeds. You'll need to opt for shallow containers with drainage holes. Sunlight or artificial lights will work with this microgreen, but we prefer artificial grow lights.

Fill your tray with soil, spread the seeds evenly, and ensure the seeds cover most or all of the soil surface. Mist the seeds with water and then cover them with another tray. Leave them for a couple of days as they will only require darkness and water. After the seeds are germinated, however, you'll need to provide them with a lot of water. From here on, you must bottom water the soil and keep repeating this step to ensure the soil remains moist. By the 7th day, your seeds will have sprouted, so you'll need to remove the tray and expose the plant to light for about 16 to 18 hours every day. The sunlight will give it its green color.

The harvest time is about 7 to 10 days. You'll know it is time when the microgreens become 2 to 3 inches tall. Make sure you harvest the plant before its leaves grow.

Carrots

Although carrots may take up to two weeks to harvest, it is still worth it due to their many health benefits. Carrots are rich in antioxidants, vitamin A, and potassium. This vegetable improves your immune system, keeps your skin hydrated, makes your hair look healthy, and protects you from diabetes. Not too shabby.

Carrot seeds don't require pre-soaking since they can easily absorb water from the soil. You'll need a growing tray with drainage holes filled with soil. Water the soil thoroughly and then smooth the surface. Then, you know the drill, spread the seeds evenly to cover all of the soil's surface. However, make sure that the seeds don't overlap. This can be tricky since carrots seeds are very small.

You may need to opt for a seed shaker to make the job easier. Make sure that you press the seeds into the soil so they will absorb the water and germinate. Now, cover your tray with another one to block out the light. They will need about four to seven days to grow and germinate. Do not remove the cover under any circumstances. The soil already has enough water, so there's no reason to take the cover off or water them.

You can finally sneak a peek after four days. If all of the seeds have started growing white shoots, it is safe to remove the cover. Expose the plant to light, preferably using an artificial grow light, for about 12 hours every day. As a result of the light exposure, the sprouts will start growing and transform to a green color. During this process, you must constantly bottom water the soil as it will require more water. Once the leaves start unfolding, they are ready to harvest. Harvest time for carrot microgreens is usually 8 to 14 days.

Cabbage

Cabbage microgreens are very popular because they have a high nutritional value since they contain various antioxidants, potassium, and vitamins A, C, and E. Cabbage seeds don't require pre-soaking, so you'll skip this step; they are already soft and small, so they will grow without soaking. You'll need a tray with drainage holes; fill almost all of it with soil (cabbage microgreens can grow in soil or hydroponically). Smooth the surface and mist it by spraying water onto it. Plant the seeds evenly over the soil's surface, and ensure they don't overlap. Next, mist the surface once more and cover your seeds with another tray.

They need to be kept away from the light and remain in the dark for 2 to 4 days. When most of the seeds finish sprouting, they will begin to push the tray cover. You'll need to remove the cover and expose the plant to sunlight for 12 hours every day. When you notice that they're changing color and looking healthier, you must bottom-water your plants once during this process.

The harvest time for cabbage microgreens is 6 to 14 days. They will be 1 to 3 inches tall and fully open with beautiful coloring. Make sure that you harvest them before the leaves grow.

Basil

There are various types of basil with different flavors, from strong and sweet to cinnamon or lemon. Basil takes a longer time to grow than other microgreens. Still, it is worth the wait since it contains healthy nutrients like minerals and vitamins A, C, and K. Basil seeds don't require pre-soaking because they will clump together. You won't be able to sow them over the soil. You probably know by now that you'll need a growing tray with drainage holes. Place the soil in the tray, then give the soil a mist of water before smoothing it out. Spread the seeds over the soil using a seed shaker since basil seeds are very small, much like the aforementioned carrot seeds. After you finish spreading the seeds, mist them a second time with the water spray. However, don't overdo it since they don't require much water. Cover the seeds with another tray for four days to block out the light and give the seeds the chance to grow.

Do not remove the cover for the duration of this period. The seeds won't need watering since the soil will have enough water to last for a few days. Take a look at the seeds on the 4th day to see how they have grown. If they have sprouted and have folded leaves, then it is safe to remove the tray. However, if they don't look ready yet, give them a water mist, cover them again, and leave them for a day or two. By that time, your plant will require light. Expose them to a grow light every day for about 12 hours so they can turn grassy green and glorious.

You'll need to bottom water your microgreens until they are fully grown. Do this process every few days. The harvest time for basil microgreens is 10 to 13 days. Unlike some of the microgreens we have mentioned throughout this chapter, you'll need to wait for the basil leaves to grow before you harvest them, and they grow about 2 to 3 inches. Let them dry before you harvest them, so avoid watering them for eight hours before harvesting.

Corn

Corn is one of the easiest microgreens that you can grow, and you can either grow it on soil or a hydroponic grow mat. This type of microgreen can be very good for your health since it contains vitamins A, B, C, E, magnesium, and calcium. It is also rich in antioxidants. Corn seeds will need to be pre-soaked for about 8 to

12 hours. However, some people prefer to leave them for 24 hours. This is up to you, but once you notice that the seeds are soft, they are ready to be planted.

As always, you'll need to fill your growing tray with soil, mist the soil so it will be moist, and then smooth the surface. Spread the seeds all over the soil surface. Mist the seeds once again before covering them with another tray. Leave them covered for about 2 to 3 days so they can grow. Exposing the seeds to any type of light during this period of time can affect the flavor and make it bitter. You'll need to bottom water it to avoid lifting the cover. You can determine if it needs water or not by the weight of the tray. If it is heavy, then there is probably enough water. On the other hand, if it is light, then the soil has dried out and requires bottom watering. By now, the corn should have light yellow shoots.

Give your plant six to seven days to grow until they become 2 to 4 inches tall. Do not let them grow over 4 inches, or they will turn bitter, harvest them right away. Usually, the harvest time for corn is between 12 to 16 days. Your plants must have light yellow leaves because if they turn green, they will be bitter.

There are many types of microgreens out there, and growing them is very easy. Once you know what each seed requires regarding light exposure, watering, and the pre-soaking time, you'll get the hang of it and be able to plant various seeds in no time, whether as a hobby or to start a business which we will cover in detail in the coming chapters. It is also worth keeping notes on all of the processes used for each type of microgreen you try to grow so you can refer to your notes and learn from them,

Chapter 4: Micro-Market Research

It's important to do your research when starting any business, and a microgreens business is no exception. When you're conducting research, it helps to understand exactly what market research is and why it's crucial for potential growth. This chapter will discuss the importance of doing your due diligence before launching a company to determine the best possible niche and pricing strategy. It will also include specific niches that could be profitable, as well as how social media and prices affect your bottom line.

What Does a Microgreens Business Entail?

Before starting a microgreens business, you must first decide what type of microgreens you want to grow. In the previous chapter, we covered the many different types and their needs. With this in mind, do your research and find the right fit for your skills and interests. You'll also need to choose a growing medium (something to grow your microgreens in) and a growing area (a space for you to grow them).

When choosing what types of microgreens to grow, you'll need to consider whether the market demand matches or exceeds the amount you are expecting. It's also helpful if there is an interest in niche varieties such as arugula, mustard greens, or pea sprouts.

While you're doing your research, make sure you assess the current market trends to estimate profit margins and growth potential for each microgreen variety. If a seedling isn't selling well now but has potential for future sales, this would be an example of the type of insight you need to have when deciding what types of microgreens your business will grow.

How Do I Start a Microgreens Business?

Once you have decided what type of microgreens to grow and have done your research on the current market trends, now it's time to start your business. The first step is to create a business plan. This document will outline your goals, strategies, and how you plan to achieve them.

Your business plan should also include a section on marketing. This is where you'll cultivate your target market, how you'll reach them, and what methods you'll use to generate sales. Social media can be a powerful tool for a microgreens businesses, so make sure to utilize it to its fullest potential.

How Do I Choose a Niche?

When choosing your niche, you want to ensure that there is enough demand for what you are selling. Look at the market trends and see how specific varieties of microgreens are trending compared to others, and adjust your plans accordingly. It can be difficult if your growing area is too small to accommodate variety. In that case, this is one thing that should be addressed in your business plan. Niche microgreens such as arugula, radish, and mustard greens may be much more successful than standard sprouts like broccoli or alfalfa seeds because you can bring them to market quicker without any major setbacks.

The First Steps

The first step to starting your microgreen business is to decide what type of growing medium you'll use. This includes pre-made units that are available for purchase or containers and materials needed to prepare your own. It's best if you can find a way to recycle as much material as possible as this will save money in the long run.

Your growing location can be a simple setup in your backyard or garage, as long as you have good ventilation and adequate light. If you're using artificial light, which some seeds require, as mentioned in the previous chapter, make sure you calculate the wattage of each bulb and how many hours of light you'll need per day.

There are several options to get your startup off the ground, but you need to do your research to ensure everything you need for a microgreens business is accessible to you, from a sufficient growing area to the right lighting. Create a business plan and assess the market trends to help you narrow down your options as well. With a little bit of hard work and dedication, your microgreens business can be very successful.

Financial Considerations and Budgeting

Launching any business can be expensive, but microgreen businesses tend to have lower startup costs than other agriculture companies. Depending on your space and resources, you may need to invest in some specialized equipment or tools. Again, this will depend on the type of medium you choose. If you're using a tray system with a soil mix or using growing plugs that you can reuse and repot, your startup costs will be less.

When you're choosing a growing area for microgreens, consider how much space you'll need per variety of seedlings or plants. A cubic foot of soil mix contains about 50-100 seeds. Basically, if each tray holds one cubic foot, that means you can plant 50-100 seeds in one tray. When thinking about how many plants to grow, you must also consider the space they will need and your budget for each variety of seedlings. This way, you won't buy too few, nor will you end up with a surplus of microgreens at the end.

Make a budget for your marketing effort, as well. Social media is the fastest way to gain traction for a microgreen business and makes it easier to connect with your customers.

One of the best ways to keep track of your expenses is by using a cash flow projection sheet. This document will help you understand how much money you are making and spending on a monthly basis. It is important to be realistic about your expenses and income, and this will help you stay on track financially.

Draw up projections for your first year of business, accounting for all income and expenses. Make projections to show how much you'll be spending on each variety of microgreens you plan to grow. It is also a good idea to make rough estimates as well because, this way, even if something unexpected comes up, you won't have to worry about it having a negative impact on your budget.

Document this budget in your business plan as it will be a valuable resource as your business grows.

Benefits of Budgeting for Your Business

Budgeting for your microgreen business is essential to get your financial affairs in order. It will help you stay realistic and organized when it comes time to make financial decisions.

As with any other small business, keeping an accurate budget can be difficult, but this is where a cash flow projection sheet can come in handy during tax season or if something unexpected happens.

This document can help you stay on top of your expenses and income, making it easier to correct any financial mistakes and reduce risk.

When you have a solid budget in place, it is much easier to make decisions about expanding your business. You may find that you need to invest in new equipment or hire more staff. Knowing how much money you have available allows you to make informed decisions that won't put your business at risk.

Budgeting also allows you to keep track of your spending habits. This information can be helpful when it comes time to file your taxes, as you'll know exactly how much money you've made and spent over the year.

A well-crafted budget is essential for any small business. When you are running a microgreen growing operation, it will be harder to manage operations if you cannot ascertain exactly how much money you'll need to spend on each aspect. Consequently, this will also make it difficult to grow your business if you don't manage the funds head-on. Poor financial management leaves too much room for error.

It will be easier to keep track of any profit with a proper budget set. If you're selling directly at farmers' markets or through social media, an accurate budget is necessary to track the earnings from each sale.

To stay organized, make sure to have a place where you can store all financial documents and receipts. You may even want to consider an online bookkeeping service. This will allow you to log in anytime from just about anywhere and check on your business finances as they grow.

Market Research

When starting a microgreens business, you must focus your attention on understanding the market for your product and investigating any competition you have. This kind of research helps you make sure you can identify and fill any void in the market and helps you gain a competitive edge.

Then, you must concentrate on knowing who your target customer is. Do some digging and figure out what needs and wants your customers have. Creating a customer profile can help you narrow down your results and build a marketing strategy that will drive more sales and attract new customers.

How to Do Market Research for Your Microgreen Business

Start by looking at the market for your product to gauge whether microgreens are already in demand. If so, what variety is most popular? Are there any other trends you can capitalize on when it comes time to launch your business?

As mentioned above, be aware of your competition. What are they selling? How much do they charge for their product? What kind of marketing strategy are they using, and are their methods effective?

Once you have a good understanding of the market, you need to figure out who your target customers are. These people may not be who you think they are. Do some research to prepare customer profiles and see if there are any untapped markets that you could explore.

Once you know your target customers, it's time to figure out what they want. What needs do these people have? How can you meet their needs with your product? What makes your microgreens stand out from the competition?

When putting together a marketing strategy, it's important to keep your target customers in mind. What would they be most likely to respond to? Are there any specific demographics you want to focus on?

It's also crucial to determine your marketing budget. How much can you afford to spend on marketing? What are the most effective channels for reaching your target customers?

Market Research Techniques for Your Microgreen Business

You can use several market research techniques when starting your microgreens business. Some of the most common include surveys, focus groups, and interviews.

Surveys offer more versatility than other methods because you have access to a larger number of people, and therefore the insight you gain will be more diverse. Create a questionnaire and send it out to potential customers or those who have already purchased your product. Have an online link to a survey to reach a wider audience.

Focus groups allow people to be more involved in market research. This is when you invite potential customers into the process of creating and testing new products. Here, you can pick their brains and gain in-depth ideas for marketing strategies and tactics from the horse's mouth.

One of the most useful market research techniques is to hold interviews. These are much more in-depth than surveys or focus groups and give you direct access to your target customer.

Note that it is not enough to focus on your market alone. It is necessary to conduct some research on the market in general. Discover what trends are happening and how you can use them to your benefit.

One of the most comforting things about starting a microgreen business is that it doesn't require a large investment to get it up and running, lowering the risks if the business doesn't take off.

Selecting a Niche for Your Microgreen Business

One of the most important aspects of market research is selecting a niche for your microgreen business. This means finding a specific group of people to target with your product.

When selecting a niche, it's important to think about what needs and wants this group has that aren't being met by other businesses. What makes your microgreens unique? What can you do to make them stand out from the competition?

Examples

If you are growing kale, one niche may be health-conscious people who want organic foods. Another may be chefs looking for a specific variety of kale that will complement their dishes and provide an interesting new flavor. A third may be people who are looking for a sustainable, eco-friendly way to buy their produce.

It's important to remember that niches can change over time. In other words, what might be a good niche today may not be tomorrow. So, it's important to stay on top of current trends and make sure your product is always relevant.

Developing Product Packaging That Appeals to Your Niche

Part of standing out among the competition is to have product packaging that appeals to your niche. This means using colors, fonts, and images that resonate with this group of people.

It's also important to make sure your branding is consistent across all platforms, from your website to your social media pages, since everything should look the same.

If you are selling microgreens as a fresh, organic product to health-conscious people, your branding should reflect that. Think earthy colors like browns and greens with natural fonts and images of healthy food.

There is no one right way to create brand consistency. What works for one person or business may not work for another, so it's important to do some research and testing.

Pricing Your Microgreens

When pricing your microgreens, you need to be accurate and thorough to ensure your business is priced fairly for customers but also provides decent cash flow. After all, this is an investment, and you need to ensure you're making a solid income.

Pricing your product can be challenging because there are many factors that go into creating an effective price. These factors include production costs, overhead expenses, transportation, and marketing budget.

You also have to consider how customers perceive your prices in relation to those of your competitors.

Below is a breakdown of some common pricing structures for microgreens. Use these as guidelines to help you determine the best course of action for your business.

- **$0-$20 Per Pound** – These prices should be used if growing in-house or buying from local growers, who are usually able to offer lower prices since they don't have to factor in transportation costs.
- **$20-$30 Per Pound** – This price range is for microgreens that are being sourced from a distance and must be transported.
- **$30+ Per Pound** – For specialty or rare microgreens, these prices can reflect the high demand and the limited supply.

(Prices for reference only)

Other Considerations for Pricing

Remember that the prices alone aren't everything. You also need to consider other factors when pricing your microgreens.

- **Your Profit Margins** – Are they high enough? It can be difficult to know without doing some research and trying to determine realistic expectations.
- **The Effect of Price on Sales Volumes** – You are probably familiar with the concept of price elasticity, which means that if your prices go up, sales will also decrease. In microgreen businesses, people who buy fresh produce tend to be more sensitive to changes in pricing. Keep this in mind when determining how much you plan to charge for each product and whether or not you'll be offering discounts.

- **The Cost of Production** – This is the amount it costs to produce a certain quantity of microgreens. Remember that you need to make some profit on each sale.

- **Packaging and Shipping Costs** – If you are selling online, you'll need to factor in the cost of packaging and shipping.

Using Social Media Marketing to Promote Your Microgreen Business

Social media marketing is an integral part of any business's promotional efforts. It can help get your brand out there, increase traffic to your website, and allow you to talk with potential customers.

Many social media platforms offer free or low-cost options (such as Facebook). However, if you want to reach a more targeted audience, you can consider using paid advertising options.

Below are some tips for marketing your microgreen business on social media:

- **Create a Strong Social Media Presence** – This means having well-designed pages with interesting and engaging content. Ensure all of your information is up-to-date, and reply to comments and messages promptly.

- **Develop a Social Media Strategy** – Decide which platforms you want to use, what type of content you'll share, and how often you'll post.

- **Use Paid Advertising Options** – This can be a great way to reach more people who are interested in your product. Target your ads to specific demographics, and make sure you are using effective keywords.

- **Engage with Customers** – Show that you care about your customers by responding to their comments and questions. This will help build trust and loyalty.

The Importance of Social Media

Social media is an excellent way to market your microgreen business, but you mustn't neglect the other types of marketing that are a necessity for growing and selling microgreens.

Make sure you do some research into which platforms work best with your target audience, especially if you plan to use paid advertising options. This will help ensure that you're getting the most out of your marketing efforts.

For instance, if all of your clients are young professionals who use social media on their mobile devices, it makes sense to have a strong presence on Facebook. But if those same customers prefer email and print advertising, then it won't be necessary for you to create an account on Instagram.

Social media has a tremendous reach and can be a very effective way to connect with potential customers. By using it in conjunction with other forms of marketing, you can create a well-rounded promotional campaign that will help your microgreen business succeed.

According to Statista, in 2021, there were about 193.9 million Facebook users in the United States alone. That is a huge market to reach.

The main thing is that you know who your target audience is and what they are doing on social media platforms where relevant people can find them. It's not just about having a Facebook page with nice pictures. It's also about engagement – the ability to add value or provide helpful information to others in a way that makes them want to come back for more.

When you are able to do this, it builds trust and loyalty among followers, who may then become paying customers.

Remember that social media is just one piece of the marketing puzzle, so be sure to use a variety of strategies to reach your target audience. By doing so, you'll increase the chances that your business will succeed.

Paid Advertising Options

If you are selling your microgreens online, then advertising on social media platforms is a great way to direct people to your products. However, if doing so isn't feasible for your business (or even necessary), there are other paid advertising options that can help get your brand out in front of potential customers.

One option is using Google AdWords, which allows you to place ads on Google search results pages. You can target your ads to specific demographics, and you only pay when someone clicks on your ad.

Another option is Facebook advertising. With this type of advertising, you can create custom audiences based on interests, behaviors, or demographics. You also have the ability to target people who live in a certain area or who have visited your website in the past.

Facebook advertising can be a great way to reach more people who are interested in your product. By targeting ads to specific demographics, you can ensure that you're reaching the right people. And by using effective keywords, you can ensure that your ad pops up when potential customers are searching for related information.

When you're advertising your microgreen business, it's highly advised to use a variety of strategies to reach as many people as possible. By using paid advertising options in conjunction with social media marketing, you can create a comprehensive promotional campaign to help your business succeed.

Micro market research is a critical process that should not be taken lightly when starting a business. This chapter has stressed the importance of doing your due diligence before starting any business, including a microgreen business. One must always consider all aspects of the business – from creating a business plan and understanding your target audience to social media marketing and using paid advertising options. By engaging with customers on social media, you can build a professional relationship and gain credibility, which could lead to sales. Social media should not be the only form of marketing used for a microgreen business. Other forms such as print, email, and targeted ads should also be considered to reach the widest range of potential customers. When done correctly, micro-market research can help launch a successful microgreen growing business and serve as a guide for potential growth.

Chapter 5: How to Grow for Fun

When you are just starting out, growing microgreens can seem like a very difficult task, one that requires a lot of skills, plenty of gadgets, and a lot of hours to look after the plants. Even though these plants are very small and delicate and sell for extremely high prices, the process of taking a seed all the way to a fully developed microgreen is relatively simple and quick. However, it does take a basic understanding of the process itself, the environment that you are raising your plants in, and the maintenance that is necessary to get your seeds to flourish.

If you end up seeing only a handful of seeds actually germinating from your first batch of a few hundred, or a few thousand, it is nothing to be surprised about and nothing to lose hope over either. This is completely normal and something that everyone faces. This is going to be very common if you haven't grown any kind of plant before and you aren't familiar with your local climate. If you get seeds from a grower who provides instructions, there will be some variation in those instructions to meet your exact requirements. Even if you are in the same city, the internal climate of your house can vary a lot from the climate used by the grower when testing the seeds.

You don't need to have the fanciest and most expensive equipment to start off with. Of course, having some good equipment will help, but it is not a necessity by any means. You can start growing in your backyard just as easily, and even though the success rate may be low at first, at least you'll understand how things work in your region.

More importantly, it does take some time to experiment with different varieties to see what works for you. Luckily, the growth cycle of microgreens is very short, and there are noticeable differences on a daily basis. Earlier in the book, it was suggested that you keep notes, and these help you to find out where you may be going wrong.

Finding the Right Seed

Nearly any kind of edible plant can be grown as a microgreen. Most experts are of the opinion that microgreens are either just as good as the fully developed versions of the plant or even better. Generally, plants belonging to the broccoli family are preferred. This includes varieties of cabbage, broccoli, kale, mustard, and cauliflower, among others. The main benefit to using the kale broccoli family is that they grow extremely quickly. You can expect a ready crop in less than a week to a maximum of ten days. These have plenty of powerful antioxidants, nutrients, minerals, and all kinds of other beneficial compounds.

If you want a bit more diversity, you can look into growing other plants such as onions, cucumbers, spinach, lettuce, carrot, leek, or Swiss chard. You'll notice that all of these plants have a pungent taste of the end product that we are used to eating, and they are all extremely delicious little plants that can be eaten on their own, unlike their fully-formed versions that need to be cooked.

Other plants that can be used as microgreens include lentils and legumes. In fact, the dried lentil and legume beans can be used to start a little tray of microgreens from peas, beans, fava beans, chickpeas, and even fenugreek. Other popular legumes that are used include sunflower seeds and flax.

If you want to use microgreens with a bit more aroma, you can use traditional herbs such as cilantro, basil, chives, cumin, or dill, among others. The great thing about using herbs is that you can harvest some when they are the size of microgreens, while you can leave the rest to fully form and eat those in due time. Luckily, the fully formed version of herbs doesn't take very long to mature, so you won't have to wait longer than a few days.

Also, when choosing the seeds, you can either stick to one kind of seed for the entire tray though it is a popular practice to mix and match seeds together to get different combinations. This is largely done for the color variations and the mix and match of textures and flavors, but this can be a bit more challenging for a new grower as you have to ensure that all of the microgreens with different needs mature at the same time. This is the process that is generally used for those bags of mixed, colorful microgreens that you see at the market. While the results are incredible, it is a tough shot the first time around.

It's also important to note that some plants are edible in their fully formed state, but that can be quite dangerous as microgreens. This is because they have high levels of alkaloids when they are at the microgreen stage, and eating just a handful of these can be quite dangerous, even fatal. Plants that should definitely be avoided include potatoes, eggplants, pepper, and tomatoes, among others. If you are starting off with a bag of microgreens, whether single seed type or mixed, you'll be fine. However, if you are selecting seeds on your own or using seeds from existing vegetables and plants, make sure they are safe to eat at the microgreen stage.

If you are allergic to any plant, even eating it at the microgreen stage can be hazardous so stay clear of these plants anyway. If you are a beginner, it is also advisable not to experiment with wild species of plants as it can be very difficult to detect the difference between edible and non-edible varieties. They can look extremely similar at that small size, and eating them at that stage can still be dangerous. For beginners, starting with something safe such as cabbage, lettuce, or herbs is better.

When sourcing seeds, it is a good idea to buy them from a reputable source for a few reasons. Firstly, you'll get high-quality seeds that won't be very difficult to germinate. You'll have a much higher success rate than by using seeds that you collect yourself. Secondly, most of the well-known seed suppliers have a dedicated list of microgreen seeds that you can look into to get seeds that produce microgreens that are safe to eat, and you can also get some that are easy for beginners. Thirdly, you can be sure that you are getting pure seeds that have not been treated with any kind of chemical and have not been tampered with in any way. Seeds that are used for microgreens need to be harvested and prepared in a specific way to ensure their microbial safety. You'll also get a lot more information about the plants you are about to grow, including details like germinability rates, germination test dates, number of seeds per pound, and some good information about the optimal growing conditions for those seeds.

Calculating the Optimal Growing Conditions

After finalizing the decision about which microgreen you want to grow and get your delivery of the seeds, the next step is to prepare the soil you want to plant them in. Whether you are looking to grow them indoors or outdoors, you'll need to prep the soil and give the seeds the environment they need. If you are starting off with a germination tray of some kind, you'll have an idea of the size of the area you are working with. If you are using an open garden, then it is a good idea to select a certain area and mark this space to measure the area in terms of square feet or square yards. This is going to be important when it comes to calculating the density of the seeds that you should use for that specific area.

Depending on the seeds you use, you'll want to spread them around at a certain density. If it is too low, you'll be wasting space, and if it is too densely populated, the goodness from the soil will be suffocated by the microgreens. By weighting out measurements, such as tablespoons full of seeds, you can quite accurately estimate how many seeds there are in each tablespoon. Then, using this measurement, you can spread the seeds around in that area according to the required density.

The Right Growing Medium

When it comes to growing microgreens, you need to narrow down what you want to grow them in and what you want to grow them with. Most people prefer to grow microgreens out of microgreen trays which are specialized plastic trays designed for this particular task. The main difference between microgreen trays and the standard nursery pots is the depth. The trays tend to be much shallower and larger, much like a tray rather than a pot where an individual plant can be isolated. Even if you are growing the plants outside, it is more efficient to grow them in trays rather than planting them directly into the earth. Microgreens are very small, and handling them when they are on the ground is rather difficult.

You don't have to get these specialized trays. However, you can use any kind of tray as long as it is food-safe and it has a few holes at the bottom for drainage. These drain holes will also come in handy when you want to water the plants, as you can dip the tray with the holes into another tray that is slightly larger and filled with water to start wetting the plants from underneath. As the medium of growth, which may be soil or a growing pad, is quite thin and the seeds are easily disturbed, wetting the tray from the bottom helps keep everything in place and avoids disturbing the environment too much. Note that you want tools that will not rust easily and that can withstand direct sunlight if you are planning on growing the plants outside.

For the growing medium, you can use regular soil mixed with some fertilizer for microgreens, or you can use a growing pad. This is a specialized pad that is set at the base of the tray and serves the same purpose as soil. There are many different pads that you can use made from various materials, including hemp, coconut husks, and others.

To make things easier, you can use any kind of tray that you have lying around the house. Simply make some holes in the base, and your germination tray is ready.

Some people prefer to use soil, which is the only option when you are planting directly in the ground.

Soil

There is absolutely no problem with planting microgreens in your backyard as long as the soil available has not been exposed to fertilizers that are not safe for food crops. Most commercial fertilizers that are designed for the grass or for regular gardening contain chemicals and additives that are not safe for human consumption. You can solve this problem by getting a soil mix that is especially for microgreens or solely for home food growing gardens.

This mixture will save you the trouble of having to infuse fertilizers and checking pH and all other technicalities. You simply pour the soil into the tray, and you're good to go. If you are using pads, it is even easier as you don't have to do anything at all other than lay the pad out and put the seeds onto the pads. If you're a first-timer, consider starting with pads. They are a lot easier to work with, and you get a much higher quality result. The problem with soil, especially when growing microgreens, is that it is very difficult to clean the microgreens later on. They are extremely close to the soil, and even the top leaves can be soiled when you pull them out.

The Right Fertilizer

For the first few times that you grow microgreens, you'll not need to fertilize the soil or introduce any additives. There is usually enough nutrition in the soil naturally to get you through at least half a dozen batches of microgreens. That is six complete cycles from seed through to the final product.

If you are using potting soil, simply get a new bag and restart the entire process when you see that germination is starting to take too long or you spot any other problems that arise from nutrition deficiencies. If you plan to use the same soil or the same pad for the long run, then there are a few fertilizers specially designed for microgreens that you can look into.

Seeding

For some seeds that have a particularly hard exterior or which are just tough seeds, you can soak them in water the night before you plan to plant them, as mentioned in previous chapters. For smaller seeds and those with softer exterior skin, you can plant them directly into the germination tray. (Refer to chapter 3 for the best seeding method based on the type of microgreens you plan to grow).

Also, when planting the seeds, it is highly recommended not to cover the seeds with soil. Simply press them down into the soil gently so that they have good contact with the soil or the pad and leave the top exposed. This will help reduce the amount of soil that you get on the leaves and the stems of the microgreen as it germinates, and this will result in a much cleaner final product. For larger seeds, you can even use another tray a little smaller and push gently against the growing medium to secure the seeds in place.

Light

Like any plant, microgreens also need plenty of light. However, the amount that is needed varies at different stages. When you first seed the microgreens, the best solution is to keep the seeds in the dark. You can cover the tray with another tray, or if you have a room that remains dark, you can put the tray in there to get the germination process started. This can take anywhere from 24 to 72 hours. Once the germination process begins and the first few shoots start to develop, you want to keep them in the dark until these shoots get to at least ¼ of an inch in height. During this time, the only thing to keep an eye out for is the water level in the growing medium and the amount of oxygen that they are getting. As they are covered or in a dark space, make sure they are getting enough ventilation, or this may encourage the growth of mold.

Once the microgreens are about half an inch tall, remove the covers and expose them to direct sunlight. For most plants, you can keep them in the sun for however many hours of sunlight you have in your region. Though be mindful of the temperatures. You don't want the microgreens getting too hot or too cold. The minimum you should allow is 50F, while the maximum should be 80F under direct sunlight. If it gets too hot, put them in the shade where they can still get sufficient light but are not in direct sunlight.

Water

The other very important thing is water. While the seeds are in the germination process, use a spray bottle to gently spray mists of water over the seeds to provide enough water while keeping their base intact and not moving them at all. The seeds only need to be kept damp on the surface. Too much water will cause mold. On the flip side, too little water will dry them out.

Once the germination has taken place, you want to minimize the contact between the green part of the microgreens and water. Ideally, you should be watering them from the bottom through the drainage holes. Depending on the humidity, the temperature, and the water consumption of the greens, you could water these plants once every two days or three times per day. Keep an eye on the growing medium and check to make sure it is damp at all times.

Common Problems with Growing Microgreens

As with anything, there are a few common pitfalls when growing microgreens and – especially as a beginner – this can be a real hassle to deal with. Ideally, if you have everything properly sorted out, such as the seeds, the soil, the lighting, and the water, there shouldn't be a problem with things like disease. However, there are a few exceptional situations where even the best preparations will not help counter the problems encountered. Here are a few solutions to two of the main issues.

• Slow Growth Rate

Some seeds are generally slower germinating than others, which means you can have various germination rates in the same batch. The problem usually comes down to a few variables, including the amount of water available to the seed, the amount of air that it is exposed to, and the temperature that the seed needs. If you give the plant too much or too little water, this can impact the speed of germination. Also, when planting in large trays, there is a chance that the water isn't evenly distributed across the terrain, so different seeds are germinating at different rates.

Sometimes people have the tray positioned in such a way that one portion of the tray receives a few extra hours of light, causing the water to dry up faster on that side. Similarly, you also want to ensure that there is enough airflow in the region. If natural ventilation isn't enough, you can always add a fan or place them in a different location. Lastly, some seeds are very sensitive to temperature. Especially if you are in a place where the ambient temperature isn't high enough or there isn't enough heat coming through the light, it can really slow down germination. Moreover, it will also impact the quality of the growth. Consider adding artificial light to provide both light and heat to the seeds.

• Large Seed Size

Another problem is size, especially for those who buy raw, ungraded seeds or who are using seeds from other fruit and vegetables that they have at home since these do not always produce a consistent size. On the other hand, there are some microgreens, such as sunflower microgreens, that just have a much larger seed size.

The problem is that the larger seed doesn't make enough contact with the ground and the growing medium and therefore doesn't receive enough water and nutrition or a base to settle into. Plus, these larger seeds require more water, and if you aren't used to planting this larger size, you may not be giving it enough water. When people plant larger seeds, they tend to sow fewer seeds, whereas, in reality, the larger seeds can be planted with the same density as the smaller seeds. This is because the larger seed size itself makes up for the lack of space. The larger seeds spread themselves out more, and this creates enough room even for microgreen plants. Just make sure the layer of soil above and below the seeds is thick enough and has enough water to help the seeds to grow.

Chapter 6: How to Grow for Business

When you are looking to set up a microgreens farm as a business, you need to think of it as an independent entity that is going to generate money rather than an operation that you are doing for pleasure. Even though you may find it really enjoyable to be growing microgreens and making money from the process, it will help you to think of it as a business that you can also enjoy for personal consumption and should avoid putting your hobby above the quality of the service you'll provide for customers. While this can be a simple side-hustle, selling the remains of your product as an extra source of income rather than prioritizing the product from a business standpoint will affect sales.

Many people who think about getting into the microgreens business spend too much money on things they don't need or too little on things they do need. For instance, even though it's perfectly fine to recycle the makeshift tray you have lying around for your business, it is much better to invest in solutions meant for this specific task. Make-shift trays are good for getting your feet wet, but these basic amenities can make the process much harder when you scale operations up.

You'll realize that when you are growing large volumes of microgreens, simply ensuring that each tray is properly watered, aerated, and spaced out while ensuring that the seeds are evenly distributed can be quite challenging. When you only have a single tray to work with, the fact that all of your focus is on that one tray can help you overcome the shortcomings of the hardware. Similarly, if you are working in a confined space, you may not need additional light or ventilation when you only have a few trays, but when you have dozens of trays stacked up above each other, sufficient light and sufficient airflow become extremely important and hard to provide.

In this section, we are going to look at some of the most effective modifications you need to make to your home setup to ensure it is suitable for large-scale business operations.

Cultivation

The cultivation of microgreens is arguably one of the most challenging parts of the process. The way you tackle the job of cultivation will, to a large extent, set the pace for the entire process and will also determine how you layout different parts of the microgreens' growth cycle. For instance, the way you manage the seeds before germination will determine how you can actually make batches that you want to grow.

When you are growing microgreens on a large scale, you'll be growing certain mixes of seeds at the same time, or you may have dedicated trays of individual microgreens that you are growing collectively. To do this, you need to manage how you are going to prepare the seeds for growing. As mentioned in previous chapters, some seeds, such as chickpeas, sunflower seeds, and other large seeds with thick husks, need to be soaked in water before they are planted. However, you need to make sure that you don't soak them for too long, or they could drown. For example, sunflower seeds need to be soaked overnight, whereas peas only need a couple of hours. Ideally, this is a part of the process in which seeds should be separated, even if you plan on growing them together.

Similarly, some seeds that take longer to germinate have different temperature, water, light, and even nutritional needs. When planting groups of microgreens together, you need to ensure that you are grouping similar kinds of plants to manage them more effectively and get the best quality result.

Packaging and Labeling

One of the main changes for people who are getting into microgreens farming for commercial purposes is how the product is finally packed and labeled. One of the most important things for the packaging is how you style this package, label it, and finally, present the final product. The good idea is to look at what your competitors are doing so that you can get some ideas as to how you can package your product, but more importantly, so you can get an idea of what not to do and how to differentiate your product when it is showcased. Similarly, the way you package your products will also impact how the customer perceives them. If you target high-end consumers who want only the best, you'll need packaging that reflects that.

Generally, the microgreen farmer sells to three main categories of clients.

> **1.** Food businesses that will use microgreens in their own products (restaurants, cafes, juice shops and so on)
> **2.** Wholesalers who will distribute these goods further
> **3.** Retail stores that will sell directly to end consumers

Many microgreen farmers tend to have different kinds of packaging depending on the clients they are preparing the products for. For instance, if you are preparing the microgreens for local customers who are going to buy the package at a local grocery store, you must ensure that your packaging meets all the safety standards, meets local regulations, and is in a format that is permitted by the grocery store you are selling through. These regulations and requirements can vary quite a lot from state to state, so be sure to check what is required in that particular vicinity. At the same time, you also want to make the packaging convenient for the buyers. Offer it in multiple quantities, making it easy to handle and easy to store.

On the other hand, if you are planning on selling directly to customers, then you'll need to look at solutions for delivery and make sure that the products can stay clean and fresh while they are transported. Whether you are shipping them to the clients yourself or using a delivery service, you need a solution that can protect the plants. Where the temperature is very hot or humid, you need refrigerated transport or a transport company who can package the products in such a way that they stay at a comfortable temperature during the transport.

Again, the longer the distances get, the more challenging this becomes. Generally, transport can be quite an expensive process, so it is only the large growers and larger companies that have a nationwide presence as it costs a lot to make this available across so many different regions. Moreover, when you have a higher demand for your product, you can consider setting up multiple growing sites, which will reduce the shipping costs and radically increase the quality of the final product that the consumer gets. Rather than growing everything at one central farm, you grow all over the country and ship to nearby localities.

If you are selling to other businesses that will be using the product in food or drinks, it is more affordable and appropriate to make bigger bags with less labeling. Generally, these clients will require larger portions or at least more frequent portions, and it is a lot easier to have a bigger bag of 5 pounds rather than ten bags of half a pound each. Also, you don't need to spend that much money on the styling of the packaging. However, the quality of the packaging should still be up to par. Some manufacturers also ship their products in a large box that has all the advertisements, logos, and other visually appealing marketing embellishments on the outside while keeping the smaller plain containers on the inside. Getting custom-made packaging can be expensive, so this is a great way for you to reduce expenses. The other main benefit is that it helps to sort things out for the client. They may not have to use all ten pounds of microgreens right away, so they can just open one bag and use that while everything else remains sealed and fresh.

However, it is a good idea to have some demarcation on the smaller bags in the box, even if they don't have any of your logos or anything to specify exactly what is in said container. Usually, restaurants have one large storage area for things like fruit and vegetables and one storage space for meats. Within the storage area, there may be hundreds of boxes of vegetables. Therefore, having a tag on your boxes will make products easy to identify, which makes their operations easier as well. Coincidently, the convenience will entice them to maintain their working relationship with you.

If you are selling directly to customers, you can give them all the packaging options you can provide, whether that is small 2-ounce bags or full 10-lb.bags. Since you are going to be responsible for shipping the bags and have complete access to the order, you can offer a lot more options. Also, certain kinds of packaging can be really expensive, so you can also give them differently priced options when choosing their packaging and allow them to choose what suits their needs. Most people who will be ordering from you directly will be ordering for personal use, so packaging is not always a priority. You can also offer special packages for people who may want to gift your products to someone or want you to send the products to someone as a gift, so it doesn't hurt to have some of those celebratory packaging options available as well.

It's also a good idea to have nutritional labels on your bags and maybe throw in a few brochures about the benefits of the microgreens and the various ways in which they can be used. This kind of marketing material is not very expensive to make, especially when you are getting it printed in bulk, but it is a really great way to make a good impression on the user and make your brand stand out.

Growing Medium

As you know by now, there are two main ways in which people go about growing microgreens, either in soil or through hydroponics. As a beginner, using soil is much easier, quicker, and more cost-effective. While the end product from hydroponics is extremely high quality, it is a complicated process and requires a lot more money in the setup of the growing facility.

In terms of growing in soil, you'll have a large variety of soils that you can use. When you are just starting out, the best option is to go for organic potting soil that has some fortified additives. In terms of pre-mixed potting soils, this will be a mix of around 80% natural ingredients such as coconut coir and peat moss together with 20% of perlite. This will give you the best start and will minimize the need for additional fertilizers.

Testing Soil

The best way to test the soil is to get a sample. To get a sample, simply dig into your soil, and collect the sample from a few inches deeper than the soil surface. Add a couple of tablespoons of the soil sample into some distilled water and stir it around to combine it thoroughly. Next, drain out all of the liquid from the mixture into a petri dish or any other kind of sterilized container. Using a simple pH stick that you can purchase at the pharmacy, place the stick into the water and let it soak for a few seconds. This will show you the pH level in the soil. Ideally, you want something between a pH of 6 and 7. Anything beyond these two extremes will hinder plant growth. It will still work, but it won't be optimum. Depending on whether the mixture is too alkaline or too acidic, you can make the appropriate changes to the soil and then repeat the process.

When you are growing plants in the same soil continuously, take regular samples of the soil to see what the condition of the soil is. This way, you can optimize how many nutrients and other additives you introduce into the soil, and it will also give you an idea of how well the plants are developing.

Sterilization

Sterilization is a big part of growing microgreens when you are growing large quantities. Some of the largest growers tend to shift towards hydroponics as it makes the sanitation of the entire process much easier to manage and maintain. The first point of contact for any unwanted bacteria is the seed itself. Ideally, you should start off with seeds that have already been treated and are safe to use. If you are uncertain, then it's best to sanitize the seeds yourself. A quick solution is to mix four teaspoons of white vinegar with four teaspoons of food-grade hydrogen peroxide into a quart of water. Stir the mixture before adding the seeds for 10 minutes.

The next things to sanitize are the trays in which you are planting. If you just have a few trays, you can wash these by hand and use the same solution you made for the seeds to scrub them down. Then wash away the mixture with some fresh water. If you have a lot of trays, however, it may be worth investing in a power washer where you can line up all the trays and just pressure wash them all in one go. You may need to put a foot on them to keep them in place or consider using weights, but it will save you a lot of time.

Composting

People who are looking to eat microgreens are in it for the flavor and the nutritional value. One of the main reasons why sterilization is so important is that these plants are too small to be exposed to pesticides and other kinds of treatments, so keeping the place clean is the only way to ensure safety. Similarly, they are also too sensitive to use any kind of commercial fertilizer, so the best way to do this is by using organic compost. You can buy premade bags of organic compost, or you can make your own at home with biodegradable kitchen scraps. Things like vegetable peels, fruit waste, and even eggshells make fantastic compost. All you need is a few feet of space in your backyard where you can dump all of these items and let them degrade with time. Then you can take this partially degraded matter and add it to your soil mix to supercharge the growing medium for your plants.

Baby Greens

One of the most challenging parts of growing microgreens is keeping everything timed properly. When you are growing for your own consumption, if a plant takes a day or two more to mature or matures a day or two earlier, it's not that big a difference, and you can easily manage this variation. However, when you are part of a supply chain and other businesses are dependent on your products, and your entire profitability is dependent on how timely your deliveries are to clients, a delay of a single day can cause quite a problem. At the same time, the time that it takes to reach the perfect condition is also very important. Any high-end retail store or chef that uses your products will want the products to be homogenous in size, taste, and appearance. Leaving the microgreens in the soil for an extra day or two can drastically change all of these characteristics, and even a little bit of maturity can result in getting to the point where they are considered baby greens rather than microgreens.

What you can do is preserve some of these more mature products and let them continue to grow for a couple of additional weeks so that they actually reach that proper baby green level, and then you can sell these as an additional product. While you won't be able to charge prices that are quite as high as the price of microgreens, it will still save your efforts from going to waste. Most people who will buy microgreens will also be interested in buying baby greens. They are also very tasty and useful, and the only difference is that these plants can be up to 8 inches tall. However, it is an alternative that you can look into for products that go beyond their maturity stage as a microgreen, whether that is because they didn't sprout soon enough or you simply produced more than you could sell in that time frame.

Common Challenges

• Rot and Mold

When you are growing microgreens in large quantities and in confined spaces, it is common for them to develop mold and rot. This is particularly challenging because once mold develops on one tray, all of the others are also at risk of infection as the mold spreads throughout the area.

This problem is common when you are growing lots of trays in a confined area and you don't provide enough ventilation. The main cause of this is an excessively humid environment, resulting in too much water and too much heat and a lack of ventilation. The first thing to do is to introduce air to the area and remove the microgreens that have been in contact with mold. Secondly, stop watering the plants and let them dry out a little bit. If possible, increase the amount of direct light exposure. If this cannot be done naturally, consider investing in an artificial lighting setup to help with this process. If you live in a humid region, then consider a solution to decrease humidity so that you can keep it at around the 50% mark.

• Excess Root Growth and Tall Greens

This is usually the case when the plants aren't getting enough light and/or there is a lack of nutrients. When you are growing lots of microgreens together, it is very easy to overpopulate the trays, resulting in the plants having to extend their roots to look for nutrients that they need. On the other hand, if some plants are growing really tall, this is because there isn't enough light available or their section of the tray isn't getting enough light, which leads them to reach for better exposure. If this is the case, consider getting some artificial light or changing the position of the tray to give the plants better access to this valuable resource. At a minimum, your plants should get at least 6 hours of good light exposure every day.

• Uneven Germination

Another common issue when you are growing large quantities of microgreens is uneven germination. This happens when the tray gets overpopulated, and you have seeds that are not in contact with the soil as a result of laying on top of each other. Bear in mind that when you are using the same soil, again and again, it starts to lose its nutritional value, and after a few batches, you'll start getting empty spots on the tray where the seeds have not germinated at all. Even if you are adding fertilizer, you may still experience this as a result of not mixing the soil well. Also, if it is a very dense tray of microgreens, you may be having trouble with getting enough airflow throughout the tray, so consider improving the ventilation. Always make sure you are getting sufficient water across the whole tray in an even manner.

Chapter 7: Growing Indoors vs. Outdoors

In this chapter, we delve into one of the main reasons microgreens are gaining significant popularity; they're easy to grow. You can either grow them indoors or outdoors, depending on your preference. So, here we focus on setting up your garden indoors versus outdoors. Different environmental factors like rainfall, temperature, humidity, wind, and moisture requirements can influence your choices. The chapter also discusses the equipment required and explains how you can create ideal conditions artificially.

Growing Microgreens Indoors

When deciding whether to grow microgreens indoors or outdoors, several factors must be taken into account. The following are some of the factors that can affect your plants when you decide to grow them indoors.

- **Space**

Space is the most important thing to consider before you grow your microgreens. The space inside your home is likely to be small compared to a garden space. Therefore, it will determine the number of plants you can grow inside. You can utilize a plant rack in your home as long as you get appropriate containers for your plants and make sure they fit the space available. Make sure the pots have holes at the bottom to allow water to drain out. Remember, surroundings and the size of the space can affect how your plants grow, so make sure the location you choose is free from human traffic but is easily accessible.

Elements like aeration are also crucial since they determine plant health. When indoors, choose an area close to windows with natural air circulation. The other aspect to consider is that some plants thrive indoors better than others. Keep this in mind when choosing your microgreens. The growth rate of crops indoors differs from the plants grown outdoors as a result of different factors. The plants outside are exposed to natural conditions, which can be favorable. On the other hand, you can create a better artificial environment inside, eliminating some of the drawbacks of outdoor gardening, which can also influence the growth of your chosen plants.

- **Garden Pests**

When you grow your microgreens indoors, you have no worries about pest issues. Different types of pests can affect your crops, especially when you grow them outside. For example, outdoor plants can be easily targeted by various predators such as bugs, caterpillars, worms, ants, and flies. This can affect productivity and the quality of output you'll get. You'll realize that indoor plants are significantly safer since you can control the environment to suit their needs.

- **Temperature and Humidity**

All plants require a specific temperature to grow. As mentioned earlier in this book, most microgreens do well at room temperature between (70 °F to 80 °F). If your indoor conditions do not provide this temperature, you can find artificial means of controlling it. In some cases, the temperatures outdoors are not within this range which makes the flexibility of the indoor environment more appropriate for your plants.

Humidity is another important factor that can determine the growth of your plants. Under normal circumstances, the humidity between 50-60% is ideal for your crops. As you are aware, too much humidity and insufficient airflow can lead to the risk of mold and other soilborne diseases. Therefore, growing indoors requires appropriate watering of plants. However, bear in mind that excessive watering can cause the rot of roots which will affect your plants. The other thing you should prioritize is keeping the environment clean.

• Lighting

All indoor plants require lighting to grow once they have germinated. You must get appropriate lights that can mimic sunlight to enhance growth. With appropriate lighting, you can enjoy all-year-round crops since the light you can provide is more consistent. The light outside may not be consistent as a result of natural factors that cannot be controlled. The other thing to note is that outdoor cropping is seasonal in most cases. For instance, few crops thrive during the winter season when temperatures are low. Stunted growth can also occur due to the lack of light during the colder months. However, an abundance of light can be detrimental too. Make sure you adjust your lighting to suit the needs of your plants.

• Soil Quality

Soil is another essential consideration whether you grow your microgreens indoors or outdoors. When you decide to grow indoors, it is a good idea to have your soil tested first so you can choose appropriate crops. The same applies to the soil in your garden. It should be tested for pH (Chapter 6 provides instructions on how to test soil). Most types of microgreens require soil that is fine-grained since it drains well. If you grow outdoors, you may need to add sand, peat moss, or coconut coir to enhance nutrient content and improve drainage in your garden.

You can also amend the soil by composting it or adding artificial fertilizers to enhance growth. However, amended soil may not be good for your plants, especially when you apply fertilizers. Try to keep your microgreens as organic as possible to avoid health concerns. Artificial fertilizers can also lead to the leaching of nutrients in the soil, which can affect plant growth.

Significance of Growing Outdoors

Growing your nutrients outdoors can be the only viable option at times. The main advantage is that the environment outside is natural, and you don't need a lot of artificial enhancements for plant growth. However, there are also certain downsides to using a natural environment since there are many things you cannot control, like humidity and temperature. Therefore, there are rules you need to follow if you choose to grow your microgreens in the garden.

- **Avoiding Strong Direct Sunlight**

  While all microgreens require sunlight to grow, each type of plant requires a different amount of sunlight. Some plants require full-on sun, while others should be grown in partial shade. As you know, different types of plants require specific needs. However, it is recommended that all plants have access to direct sunlight when necessary. So, choose the location in your garden wisely.

- **Plant Microgreens in Your Garden's Soil**

You can grow your microgreens on the ground, just like other types of vegetables. However, since microgreens grow faster compared to other types of plants, make sure your plants have access to all the requirements they need, as this can ensure that they stay healthy as they grow.

Growing your microgreens outdoors can be an excellent option if you have a garden since there are also many advantages. One of the biggest advantages of growing outside is unlimited space. As mentioned above, growing indoors may not allow for sufficient space for many plants.

Advantages of Growing Outdoors

Growing microgreens outdoors has many advantages that can help you enjoy better yields at a lower cost. The following are some of the benefits of setting up your garden outdoors.

- **Less Equipment Required**

You eliminate the need for critical equipment required for growing microgreens inside your home. When you grow them indoors, you need a special source of light to enhance growth, and this kind of lighting can be expensive. But, when you grow them outdoors, you won't experience these issues. You may also need a dehumidifier to maintain appropriate levels of humidity when you grow your microgreens inside your home. Additionally, you must constantly monitor the crops grown indoors to make changes accordingly.

Another benefit of growing in the garden is that you can plant the seeds directly into the soil. There will be no need to transplant the seedlings once they germinate. There is enough space in the garden to help you to move freely. Additionally, plants in the garden can get full aeration.

• Affordability

Growing plants outdoors is generally affordable since it does not require elements like trays, other growing mediums, and paying high electricity bills. Artificial equipment like lighting and dehumidifiers require electric power to function, which will increase your monthly electricity bills. When you grow your microgreens outside, you don't encounter these challenges. All the things you need to apply indoors are readily available naturally outdoors.

You don't need to set an artificial light source outside since it comes from the sun. There are also other operational costs involved when you grow your microgreens indoors. For instance, maintenance is required for artificial equipment used for cropping indoors. You don't experience these challenges when you plant in your garden. Even when you decide to set up a greenhouse, it is cheaper to maintain since it does not require any additions. Just make sure the greenhouse has sufficient ventilation, and you locate it in an appropriately sunny or well-lit area.

• Eliminates the Need for Constant Cleaning and Watering

When you grow your microgreens indoors, you must constantly clean the space. Water coming from the plants can stain the floor, which means you'll be cleaning it up regularly. However, when you grow outside, you don't have to worry about cleanliness to that extent. All you need to do is to keep the place free of weeds. A greenhouse can play a crucial role in keeping all the unwanted elements at bay. Ensure that it is free of pests and is kept clean if you want to reap maximum benefits.

When you grow outside, you can use a drip irrigation system that provides water to the plants without any further intervention. You can install an automatic timer that can operate the system even when you are not around. However, when you plant your microgreens indoors, you need to water them more often. You may need to be available for more of the time to check on your plants. This is not the case when you choose the outdoor option. It gives you flexibility since the crops aren't as reliant on you.

How to Grow Your Microgreens Outdoors

You can only grow microgreens outdoors if you are satisfied with the climate. The ideal time to grow these plants is in late spring to early autumn, when the temperatures are suitable to support growth from seedlings to the harvesting period. Before planting, make sure your soil is good and well-prepared.

Planting

One major benefit of microgreens is that they are very easy to grow. When you decide to grow them in the garden, create raised beds. Alternatively, you can use appropriate containers. Before you grow the microgreens in the garden, first loosen the soil with a rake and remove all unwanted elements that can affect growth. Scatter the seeds over the area, and remember you'll harvest them when they are still very young, so they may not need a lot of space. Once you scatter the seeds, make sure you cover them with about 1/8 inch of soil. Gently water the bed to moisten the soil and promote plant growth.

If you want to plant your seeds in a container, choose something that is at least 2 inches deep and ensure it has a large diameter. Fill the container with good-quality soil and scatter the seeds. Make sure they are about 1/8 to 1/4 inch apart and cover them with 1/8 inch of soil. Water the soil to moisten it. You should place your containers in a spot where they can access about four hours of sunlight every day. For effective growth, make sure your plants get sufficient light, but it should not be excessive for some varieties.

Using a Greenhouse

You can create a perfect environment for your microgreens by erecting a greenhouse that gives you an ambiance similar to indoor conditions. The only difference will be the light source since a greenhouse uses natural light. This makes a greenhouse cost-effective since the source of light is free. However, the only challenge is that you cannot control the light intensity that affects plant growth. The other issue is that it is difficult to control weather conditions.

One good thing about controlled light indoors is the consistent growth of the plants. This means that you can get a high yield with better quality compared to outdoor cropping. Microgreens in a greenhouse will be standing upright, which makes them easy to harvest. Another benefit of using a greenhouse is that it helps keep pests and other foreign elements at bay. With this option, you'll not need to apply pesticides to your crops which can affect their health. You also have more control over different elements that can impact plant growth.

When choosing a place to locate your greenhouse for microgreens, make sure you choose an even surface with loose soil. This will give you better drainage and is also likely to influence positive results. Crumbly and fine soil can also be good for your microgreens since you can add compost. If you are not sure about the quality of soil or not comfortable testing it yourself, you can take it to a laboratory for testing. When your soil is tested, you'll be in a better position to know what you can do to improve it. If possible, do not add artificial fertilizers to your garden unless absolutely necessary. Try to keep your microgreens organic for excellent results.

Microgreens and Direct Sunlight

Microgreens usually require about four to eight hours of light per day. Direct sunlight is an option, but if you don't keep your plants watered and well-ventilated, then the sunlight can basically bake them. To keep them cool, consider using a net.

The better option would be indirect sunlight, especially if there is a net to filter the light. The sun's rays cause ultraviolet radiation, which can improve your plants' antioxidant properties and help strengthen the plant's resistance to certain types of diseases.

However, ultraviolet light can cause wilting if your plants are not strong enough. With microgreens, there is a limit on the amount of light they should get. Too much or too little can cause the plants to dry. They can sustain ultraviolet light for a short period, so you must keep them hydrated. Additionally, make sure the plants are in a well-ventilated area with excellent air circulation. When you plant indoors, make sure the trays are in a place with quality ventilation.

Observe the plant leaves to determine how they are faring. If the leaves appear to be wilting or curling, move the plants to a shaded area. If the microgreens are in the garden, provide shade. Again, you can always get an appropriate net to cover the plants. Dark spots on the leaves also indicate that you are overexposing your crops to direct sunlight. This may affect quality in the long run, so you should take immediate action to protect them.

If you feel uncomfortable on a hot, sunny day, it means your microgreens may also be struggling. You need to keep the crops hydrated to prevent issues like moisture stress and wilting. You can consider drip irrigation to keep the plants hydrated. Another advantage of this irrigation system is that water does not land directly on the leaves, which can lead to disease.

Maintenance

If you choose to grow microgreens in the garden, there are different measures you need to take to keep up with maintenance. You must ensure that your plants get adequate watering. You should water the crops in the morning or evening and avoid doing it in the afternoon. Remember to avoid overwatering your plants at all costs! Waterlogging can cause challenges like rotting roots or lead to stunted growth. On the other hand, never let the soil dry out if you want to keep your plants in good health.

You should not apply water directly to the plant leaves since this can lead to the formation of mold and other diseases. The type of soil in your garden will determine the amount of water you should apply to the plants. Make sure there is good drainage in your garden to prevent issues like waterlogging. You can improve the quality of drainage by amending the soil with compost. If you have rich soil in your garden, you'll not need to add fertilizer which can impact the quality of output.

Remove any weeds from your garden, so the microgreens don't compete with them for nutrients and water. You can also add appropriate mulch to your garden to help retain moisture in the soil. You should first mix granular organic fertilizer with the soil used if you plant in containers. As you know, microgreens usually grow over a very short period, so they are rarely bothered by disease and pests. However, note that if you include brassicas in your garden, you can experience the challenge of cabbage worms. In this case, consider adding a floating cover to protect them. Inspect your garden regularly and keep it free from all unwanted elements for maximum results.

Microgreens are easy to grow when you have the right knowledge and supplies since they do not require a lot of expense or time. You can grow these types of plants throughout the year indoors once you master the basic tenets of growing them. Although it is possible to grow microgreens outside, you'll realize that your harvest will be smaller. Factors like direct sunlight usually affect the growth of your plants. Additionally, outdoor conditions can also impact the texture and flavor of the microgreens. To improve your yield, choose an appropriate space in your yard that offers the best environment for growth. Last, remember how vital space is, as this is one of the challenges you can encounter if you want to grow your microgreens indoors.

Chapter 8: When and Where to Sell

With your growing process perfected and all your variables sorted out, you need to start thinking of the other important aspect of business which is selling. Getting the sales process started is often the most challenging part of the business. Once you get the ball rolling, it has a snowball effect if you keep giving it the attention that it needs. Some businesses start off strong but, due to various factors, see a decline in sales and eventually close. However, countless examples of extremely successful businesses have made a place for themselves and have remained in the industry for decades. So, in this chapter, let's go through some of the most important things that you need to know when it comes time to sell your products.

Explore Your Market

Understanding your clients, your own capabilities, and how you can bridge the gap between these two things is the key to success in this business. The main thing to note is whether there is a unique opportunity in the field from which you can profit. You may find that there are a host of microgreens that are unique to your region, which is in high demand – without enough supply. You may find that there is a certain kind of imported microgreen variety that people are producing locally, and you can focus on that. On the other hand, there may be demand in a region close to you that isn't getting enough supply and, instead of focusing on your locality, you could focus on that region.

Similarly, in nearly every market, there are those microgreens that are the cash crop, and there are those that are high-value items. Some businesses prefer to focus on sales volumes rather than on profit margins, whereas others want to have higher margins even if that means sacrificing long-term sales. The style that you choose will influence how your business grows and how you market that business. Ideally, you should use a mix of both these high-running items as well as the high-profit items to get a feel for the market and see what direction you want to pursue.

You may also notice that different seasons of the year are naturally better for growing certain kinds of microgreens. So, you can also modify your selling approach according to the time of year and what is most convenient for you to grow. The biggest microgreen farmers have completely custom-built facilities where they can eliminate the influence of external factors entirely and create the exact environment they need to foster growth for their products. While this is a highly effective solution, it is quite costly and not possible for people who are just starting out.

Marketing

Regardless of how good your crop is, the first thing that you'll need to do is to get started with some form of marketing. This is simply about getting the word out about your business, letting people know that you exist and you are willing to sell. There are a few different ways that you can do this, and we will look at two main approaches. However, in terms of reach, you want to start with the people that are closest to you and slowly work your way toward broadening your customer reach. Think of yourself as the center point and all the people that you know and the general population as people around you. You want to start from the innermost circle and work your way toward the larger audience.

Online

Online marketing, specifically digital marketing, is the easiest and the most economical way to start. There are so many things that you can do completely for free, and you can do them yourself to draw attention to your business. One of the best things to do is set up a business account with Google, list yourself on the Google maps service, start a Facebook page, and start pages on all the social media platforms commonly used in your area. At the same time, it pays to join groups that are related to your business and start following people who are well known in this industry. If you have a bit of investment, consider hiring a professional to put together your website though there are a lot of free tools at your disposal that allow you to build your site yourself. You need to pay for the hosting and the domain name if you decide to buy one.

Next comes the content. With this big online presence, you need to include material that actually engages the audience on each platform. There are many different types of content that you can create and an endless number of different ways that you can do this. In the beginning, you can create your own material and see how that performs and when you gain some traction, you can look into hiring a professional to manage this part.

Offline

The most common way to get noticed in offline marketing is simply by relying on word of mouth. Send out a message or an email to all your friends and family and let them know that you have just launched a business and are open for orders. Let everyone in your neighborhood know, maybe put up a few banners at the local shops and cafes, and even consider handing out flyers in your neighborhood or the area that you want to target. The more money you have, the larger your reach will be. A great way to get a lot of engagement with very little investment is to publish an ad in your local newspaper, your local gardening magazine, or a health journal. This quick form of marketing will get you your initial few sales and get people talking about you. You can ask your friends and family to share testimonials, which will entice people to buy your produce – just to check out what you are offering.

In both these cases, the important thing is to continuously market your business. Nothing is going to happen with just one email or just one publication on your social media. You need to be consistently putting the message out there for at least the first year. Ideally, you'll start seeing results within the first quarter, but if it takes longer, just hang in there.

Selling

When it comes to selling your products, the best tactic is to target people who can help you sell and also target the end consumers directly. There are a few different ways you can do this:

Grocery Stores

Chances are your local grocery store is already selling microgreens and is working with someone. However, there is no harm in going to find out whether they would be interested in hosting your products as well. As a new entrant, the best thing you can do for them is to offer a better margin on your product. If they are earning a dollar in profit from others, offer them an additional fifty cents. You need to stand out to incentivize them to host your products. Grocery stores get a lot of footfall, and if they are already selling microgreens, they already have a customer base. If you can get your product onto their shelves, you'll have access to not only people who are already familiar with the product but people who are interested and willing to buy it.

Farmers Markets

Your next stop should be the local farmer's market. This is a great place to be because it is where you'll find most of your competition and most of your clients. Whether that is a group of people who are there to buy their weekly groceries or the head chef of the city's best restaurant, everyone and anyone who is serious about good quality produce will visit the farmers' market. This will also give you the opportunity to interact with other microgreen farmers and see who you are up against, what they are doing, and how they are tackling the situation. The great thing is that starting up a stall in a farmers' market is not very expensive, and it is an already established market, so you benefit from the footfall. You just need to be there consistently every week to cement your position.

Direct Sales

Another technique is to reach out to customers directly. Whether that is business clients or private consumers, getting direct access to them gives you an edge. In both farmers' markets and grocery stores, your products are lined up against several other similar products, and the consumer has the opportunity to compare your offering and then make a choice. When you are able to convince a client for direct sales, you have all their attention, and they will be much more willing to make the purchase. The trick is actually finding people who will buy direct – and then actually selling the goods. The marketing that you do both online and offline should be focused on getting direct sales.

Roadside Sales

Another approach is to simply set up a stall at the side of a road, at the local park, or at any other location and start selling. All you need to do is display your products and attract the attention of passersby. After all, everyone that is passing by could be a potential customer. When it comes to roadside sales, the location is very important. For instance, setting up a stall in the middle of a very busy area may sound like a good idea, but if that is a business center, it is unlikely that anyone will want to do their grocery shopping when they are in the middle of work. Similarly, if it is an extremely busy road but one where people can't stop to shop, that won't do much good either. You want a place where there is pedestrian traffic and a place where you can find people who are in the mood to buy groceries. Suburban settings work well for this. However, you compromise your rates and reputation as people don't expect a roadside stand to be the best quality and will therefore be less willing to pay premium prices for your products. However, you do get the advantage of impulse buying and the opportunity to meet your clients directly.

Scaling Up

All of these strategies for selling can be scaled up. For instance, you can just target more grocery stores, you can work harder on direct selling, or you can have more roadside stands and open them more frequently, etc. However, there is a smarter way to scale up, and that is through synergy. Rather than bearing the brunt of the work, why not access bigger sellers and expand your network?

Restaurants

Restaurants and other food businesses need microgreens on a frequent basis, and they use large amounts. Rather than selling to a hundred individual clients, you could focus on selling to ten restaurants and make the same amount of profit. The main thing is getting your foot in the door. Also, you may have to offer a slightly lower price, but the volume will easily make up for it. Moreover, you are guaranteed a sale every day, which takes away a lot of the stress.

Retail Chains

Grocery stores are great, but retail chains are even better. If they like the product and it is a profitable option for them, you'll have no problem getting a retail chain to offer your products. This way, you'll get much better representation when your goods are being sold in stores all over the city and possibly the country. Again, this is the business-to-business sale that relies on volume and reduces the need to constantly find new clients and to think up new marketing schemes.

Distributors

For nearly all products, there are wholesalers and distributors. The job of this business is to simply reach out to clients and provide them with the goods that they need. If you can get a good distributor to stock your products, you can get a regular client who will buy things in large quantities. As long as there is a demand for your product, the distributor will be happy to pick up your product, keep their share, and forward it on to clients. This saves you the trouble of finding clients and dealing with logistics. Again, you'll have to work out a better price than the market price, but it will be well worth it considering the fact that you'll be working less. Also, you get access to the distributor's entire network, so it serves as a great way to market your products as well.

Optimization

The one thing that will be an ongoing activity in the sales department is optimization. Whether that is marketing strategy optimization, sales strategy optimization, improving logistics, or anything else, there is always ongoing work. The market is constantly changing; to make the most of every opportunity that presents itself, you need to be on your toes and ready to cater to all these changes. One strategy will not last forever, so be sure to constantly update your systems so you are always making the most out of the circumstances you are in.

Chapter 9: Microgreen Recipes

In the previous chapters, we mentioned all the steps needed to start a profitable business by growing and selling your own organic microgreens. Now it's time to talk about how you can incorporate these microgreens into your daily meals. You can use them as the main ingredient in your mixed salads or as a garnish to a variety of dishes. In any case, the addition of microgreens is both nutritious and eye-pleasing. You can create the perfect presentation by adding a few leaflets of microgreens onto your main dishes, appetizers, salads, or even healthy smoothies. In this chapter, we offer a variety of delicious recipes to enjoy microgreens.

Beef Burger with Microgreens and Crumbled Feta Cheese

This scrumptious burger recipe is fast and simple, and the addition of microgreens instead of the regular go-to greens like lettuce goes really well with the savory feta cheese. Instead of the typical condiments such as mayonnaise or ketchup, we're going to include a simple, refreshing aioli recipe that takes this dish to the next level. There are a few things to keep in mind when cooking the meat. First, you need to be gentle when you form the patties to avoid creating a dense texture. It is also best to keep your patties in the fridge until it's time to cook them to prevent the fats from sticking to your hands. You also want to reserve the fat content in the patties to create a juicy burger. We're going to include some pickled onion slices to add a tangy flavor and crunchy texture to the burger. This recipe makes three burgers and should take a total of 25 minutes to prepare from start to finish.

Ingredients

To prepare the pickled onions:

- ¼ cup apple cider vinegar
- ½ red onion slices
- ¾ teaspoon salt
- 1 tablespoon sugar

To prepare the aioli:

- 1 clove of garlic
- ½ teaspoon salt
- ½ ripe avocado
- 1 tablespoon lemon juice
- ½ cup mint leaves
- ⅛ teaspoon ground mustard

To prepare the burger:

- 1 pound beef
- ¾ teaspoon salt
- Dash of freshly ground black pepper
- ½ tablespoon unsalted butter
- ½ tablespoon olive oil
- ¼ cup crumbled feta cheese
- ¼ cup microgreens
- 3 brioche buns
- ¾ tablespoon chipotle sauce

Directions:

1. To prepare the pickled onion, cut the onion into thin slices and place them in a jar. Then, mix the vinegar with salt and sugar in a small bowl until completely dissolved. Pour the mixture over the onion slices and set aside for an hour.

2. To prepare the aioli, mix all the ingredients together in the blender at high speed until a smooth sauce is formed.

3. To prepare the burger, form the patties to a thickness of one inch without overworking them. Press the center of the patty gently to reserve its flat shape during cooking. Keep the patties in the fridge until it is time to cook them in the skillet.

4. To prepare the brioche buns, preheat the oven to 350°F. Spread a thin layer of chipotle sauce on all the buns to give it a little heat, which works great in the overall flavor. Toast the buns in the oven for 4 to 6 minutes until golden brown.

5. On a skillet over high heat, add the olive oil and then melt the butter. Cook the patties for 6 minutes on each side for medium-rare or 8 minutes for medium.

6. Allow the patties to rest away from the heat before assembling the burger.

7. Spread the aioli on the bottom bun, add the burger patty, a few pickled onion slices, some crumbled feta cheese, and a handsome amount of microgreens, and serve.

Strawberry Chocolate Tart with Basil Microgreens

This recipe may seem like a mismatch as you may be thinking, "How can you put microgreens on a dessert?" Well, did you know that you can eat the strawberry stems along with the strawberries? Not only is this a waste-free option, but it is also proven to relieve joint pain due to its caffeic acid content. If you can eat the stems of a strawberry, you can definitely add some basil microgreens as a topping for a fresher flavor and add nutritional value to your dessert. Basil goes great with the strawberry flavor, not to mention it takes the presentation to the next level.

Ingredients:

To prepare the crust:

- 2 cups almond flour
- 2 tablespoons cocoa powder
- ½ cup coconut oil, melted
- 1 teaspoon salt
- 4 tablespoons maple syrup

To prepare the filling:

- 3 ounces goat cheese
- 2 tablespoons maple syrup
- 4 tablespoons Greek yogurt

For garnish:

- 3 cups strawberries
- 1 cup basil microgreens

Directions:

1. To prepare the crust, mix the almond flour and salt in a large bowl.

2. Pour in the maple syrup and coconut oil onto the almond flour and whisk until a dough is formed. It should be crumbly because of the grainy almond flour.

3. Add the dough to a pie pan and use a fork to create tiny holes in the crust to prevent it from bubbling up, and then place the pan in the fridge for half an hour.

4. Preheat the oven to 350F, and then bake the crust for 15 minutes until its color starts to turn brown. Set aside to cool.

5. To prepare the filling, simply blend all the ingredients in the blender until smooth.

6. Add the filling on the crust, garnish with strawberry slices, top it with a handful of basil microgreens, and serve.

Microgreen Salad

This salad is easy, effortless, and absolutely delicious. It goes really well with any type of protein and is perfect for a refreshing lunch. Feel free to add any seasonal vegetables and fruits as they go great with microgreens. You don't need to prepare a special salad dressing. A squeeze of half a lemon, some olive oil, and a dash of salt is all you need to enhance the flavor of this amazing salad. This makes a great vegetarian salad if you add some crumbly feta cheese or could be turned into a vegan option by adding some chickpeas.

Ingredients:

- 1 cup microgreens
- ½ cup grated beets
- ¼ cup thinly sliced radish
- ½ cup chopped pears, berries, or any seasonal fruit of your choice
- ½ cup sliced cherry tomatoes
- ¼ cup pumpkin seeds
- ¼ cup crumbled feta cheese
- Dash of sea salt

- Lemon juice and olive oil for the dressing

Directions:

1. In the serving bowl, place the microgreens first as a base and then neatly arrange the chopped fruits and cherry tomatoes.

2. Add the radish and beet slices all over the bowl, then sprinkle the feta cheese and pumpkin seeds on top.

3. Squeeze half a lemon on top with a drizzle of olive oil and a dash of salt. You could add all of these ingredients to a mason jar and shake them vigorously for a few seconds to create a smooth emulsion instead before pouring it all over the salad.

Microgreen Smoothie

This delicious smoothie is amazing to get your microgreen nutrients for the day while on the go. It takes under 5 minutes to prepare as you easily add all ingredients to the blender to create your smoothie. You can mix and match the additional ingredients and add your favorite seasonal fruits.

Ingredients:

- 1 ripe banana
- 3 cups microgreens
- 1 tablespoon chia seeds
- 1 cup orange juice
- 1 pineapple slice
- Ice cubes, optional

Directions:

Blend all the ingredients in the blender until smooth. You can add a tablespoon of honey to add some sweetness.

Microgreen Chutney

This recipe is amazing with some naan or pita bread for a quick snack or as a side to the main dish. It is a refreshing dip and is suitable for many occasions. You can make it for your next family gathering or house party accompanied by a few toasted bread slices and some vegetables. It only takes a few minutes, and you can stick it in the fridge to enjoy it later.

Ingredients:

- 2 cups chive microgreens
- 2 green chili peppers
- 1 cup fresh cilantro
- 2 teaspoons lemon juice
- 2 teaspoons chaat masala
- 2 teaspoons salt
- 1 teaspoon cumin
- Water

Directions:

Blend all the ingredients in the blender or food processor until combined. Be careful when you add the water to avoid a runny texture. It should be thick enough to be soaked or carried by the Naan bread. You can use any type of bread as a vessel for this dip.

Mix Cheese Pizza with Microgreens

Microgreens make a great pizza topping, giving it an amazing freshness and a wonderfully colorful appearance. One look at this lovely garden on top of the mixed cheeses will have you salivating. You'll want to make this pizza again and again as it is simple and mouthwatering.

Ingredients:

To prepare the dough:

- ¾ cup lukewarm water
- 2 ½ teaspoons dry active yeast
- 1 teaspoon salt
- 3 tablespoons olive oil
- 2 cups wheat flour
- 1 tablespoon honey

To prepare the filling:

- 1 cup ricotta cheese
- 1 cup grated parmesan cheese
- 4 tablespoons olive oil
- ¼ cup pine nuts, roasted
- ½ teaspoon salt
- 1 teaspoon ground black pepper
- Bacon strips
- 1 cup microgreens

Directions:

1. To prepare the dough, mix the water with the honey and yeast and let it sit for 5 minutes until bubbles start to appear on the surface. Then, add the olive oil.

2. Mix the dry ingredients in another bowl and then add them to the wet ingredients.

3. Mix the ingredients with your hands until a smooth dough is formed.

4. Place the dough in a warm area until it doubles in size. This can take from as little as 30 minutes to an hour or two, depending on the climate. Punch the center of the dough. You can wrap the bowl with plastic wrap and store it in the fridge for later use or use directly. This dough is enough for two pizzas.

5. Preheat the oven to 350°F.

6. Sprinkle some corn flour in the pizza pan before spreading the dough.

7. Mix the ricotta and parmesan cheese with olive oil, salt, and pepper.

8. Place the mixture on the dough and add the bacon slices.

9. Bake the pizza for 15 to 20 minutes or until the dough turns brown.

10. Add some roasted pine nuts and a handful of microgreens on top, and serve.

Roasted Potatoes with Chive Microgreens

This hearty recipe is the ultimate comfort food that works as a great side to a nice steak or grilled chicken breasts, and it can even be enjoyed on its own. It takes less than 30 minutes to prepare and is a recipe that you'll definitely want to make again. Top it with a bunch of garlicky microgreens, which is the greatest addition to these delicious roasted potatoes.

Ingredients:

- 6 large potatoes
- 2 tablespoons olive oil
- 1 teaspoon minced garlic
- Dash of salt
- Dash of black pepper
- 6 sage leaves
- 3 tablespoons unsalted butter
- Chives microgreens

Directions:

1. Preheat the oven to 400℉.

2. Wash the potatoes and then cut them into even cubes. Make sure they are not too big in size to reduce the cooking time.

3. Add the salt, pepper, olive oil, half the sage leaves, and garlic onto the potato cubes and mix.

4. Spread the potato cubes evenly on a baking sheet, and then bake for 30 minutes until golden brown. You may need to turn the potato cubes over after 15 minutes for even roasting.

5. Meanwhile, melt the butter in a saucepan over medium heat. Add the other half of the sage leaf when the butter starts to bubble.

6.Let the butter turn brown and allow the sage leaves to become crispy but be careful not to burn the butter.

7.Remove the saucepan from the heat once the butter turns golden brown. It should have a nutty smell and a caramelized color.

8.Top the potatoes with a handful of chive microgreens and serve.

Garlic Microgreens Pesto Sauce

This is a great alternative to the traditional pesto while still reserving its traditional basil flavor. The garlic microgreens give it a nice kick that makes all the difference. You'll want to grow your own garlic microgreens to make this recipe again and again. It is a healthy sauce option and suitable for vegans, which is an added bonus! You can fashion this delicious sauce in under 10 minutes.

Ingredients:

- ½ cup garlic microgreens
- ½ cup pine nuts
- ¼ cup nutritional yeast
- 1 cup basil leaves
- 1 teaspoon lemon juice
- ½ cup olive oil
- ½ teaspoon salt

Directions:

1. Mix all the ingredients in the food processor except for the olive oil until they form a paste.

2. Add the olive oil gradually until you reach the desired consistency. It should not be too runny or too thick.

3. Use this sauce on cooked pasta or as a dip with some toasted baguette slices.

Shrimp Bites with Microgreen Guacamole

This tasty appetizer is so quick and easy to make and is the perfect option when you want to entertain guests. It seems like a fancy appetizer, so this is the go-to recipe to impress just about anyone for any event. The garlic microgreens make the perfect pairing with guacamole. You'll want to include it every time you make your regular guac recipe.

Ingredients:

To prepare the shrimp:

- 1 pound peeled shrimps
- 2 cucumbers, thickly sliced
- 1 teaspoon seafood spices
- 1 tablespoon olive oil

To prepare the guacamole:

- 1 ripe avocado
- 2 tablespoons chopped fresh cilantro
- 1 tablespoon garlic microgreens
- 1 tablespoon lemon juice
- 1 teaspoon salt

For garnish:

- Garlic microgreens
- Chopped cilantro
- Cilantro microgreens

Directions:

1. To prepare the shrimp, mix it with the seafood spices and olive oil until fully covered.

2. In a medium skillet over medium heat, cook the shrimps for 2 minutes on each side and then take them off the heat.

3. To prepare the guacamole, mash the avocado and mix in the chopped cilantro, garlic microgreens, salt, and lemon juice until combined.

4. Assemble the appetizer by spreading the guacamole on the cucumber slices, top them with one shrimp each, garnish with mixed microgreens and cilantro, and serve.

Roasted Squash and Microgreens Salad

This refreshing salad pairs up nicely with your main dish or could be enjoyed on its own for lunch or dinner. It goes really well with a basic balsamic vinaigrette that gives it a tangy taste to enhance its freshness. It's a great recipe to enjoy some microgreens, which soak up the salad dressing very well.

Ingredients:

To prepare the balsamic dressing:

- 2 tablespoons balsamic vinegar
- 1 tablespoon thyme leaves
- ¼ cup olive oil
- 1 tablespoon honey
- 1 teaspoon sea salt
- ½ teaspoon ground black pepper

To prepare the salad:

- Microgreens
- Corn
- Squash
- 1 acorn squash
- 1 tablespoon olive oil
- Salt and pepper, to taste
- Garlic salt, to taste

Directions:

1. To roast the squash, preheat the oven to 350°F.
2. Cut the squash into wedges, drizzle the olive oil, and season with salt, pepper, and garlic salt.
3. Bake in the oven until soft and browned on the sides.
4. In a serving bowl, place the microgreens to form a base and then neatly place the roasted squash and acorn squash on top.

5. Drizzle the balsamic vinaigrette over the salad and serve.

Chives Microgreen Bread

This recipe is a wonderful way to make use of your grown microgreens in the garden. There is nothing better than baking a loaf of bread to enjoy over dinner. This pull-apart bread can be paired with your favorite dips, or you could use one of the sauce recipes mentioned in this chapter. It takes about 40 minutes to prepare and is enough for 8 to 10 people. You'll want to make this recipe for your dinner parties or during the holiday seasons.

Ingredients:

For the bread:

- 5 cups all-purpose flour
- 1 teaspoon salt
- 2 packets instant yeast
- 1 cup warm milk
- ⅔ cup warm heavy cream
- 3 tablespoons honey
- 2 tablespoons butter
- 1 large egg, at room temperature

For the garlic butter:

- 8 tablespoons butter
- 3 minced garlic cloves
- ½ cup grated parmesan cheese
- 3 tablespoons chopped parsley
- 1 tablespoon chopped garlic microgreens
- 1 tablespoon chopped sage leaves
- 1 tablespoon chopped thyme leaves
- Pinch of salt

Directions:

1. To prepare the dough, mix the flour with the yeast and salt in a stand mixer or by hand.

2. Gradually add the milk, heavy cream, eggs, butter, and honey while stirring continuously.

3. Cover with plastic wrap for half an hour at room temperature.

4. To prepare your garlic butter, mix all ingredients together in a bowl and set aside.

5. Take the dough out of the bowl and place it on a lightly floured surface and divide it into quarters.

6. Roll each quarter into a rectangle and spread some garlic butter on top.

7. Cut each rectangle into three long strips of dough and cut each strip into four squares.

8. You should have 12 squares of dough slathered with garlic butter for each rectangle.

9. Lightly butter a tube pan and place the squares round and round until the pan is filled with the dough squares. The squares should be placed upright and not laid down like layers. Make sure you leave some gaps between the dough squares.

10. Cover the pan with plastic wrap and allow it to rise once more for about an hour.

11. Preheat the oven to 350°F for 10 minutes. Place the tube pan in the oven and bake for 40 minutes until golden brown.

12. Allow the pan to cool down before moving it to allow it to hold its shape.

13. You can add some more garlic butter and chopped microgreens to add freshness and create a richer taste. This bread is suitable as an appetizer for dinner parties, or you can enjoy it by itself as a snack.

Here, we mentioned a few easy-to-follow recipes with microgreens that you can try at home. You can mix and match the salad recipes as you want and add seasonal fruits and vegetables to accompany your microgreens. This versatile ingredient can be added to pretty much anything from salads and appetizers to main dishes – and even to desserts.

Chapter 10: Microgreens FAQs

What Are Microgreens?

"Microgreen" is an umbrella term that describes a plant's state rather than a single plant. Any kind of vegetable plant can be a microgreen. This is defined as a plant that is less than 3 inches tall, and that has developed a true leaf. Many microgreens are also used before they develop a true leaf. Depending on the requirements of consumers, this can be a plant that can be consumed at different sizes, and it will still be considered a microgreen as long as it is smaller than 3 inches in height.

What Is the Difference between Microgreens and Sprouts?

The most notable difference between microgreens and sprouts is that sprouts are grown in water through hydroponics, whereas microgreens are traditionally grown in soil though they can be grown in water as well. Secondly, sprouts only have seed leaves, whereas microgreens are left to mature until they develop true lives. Also, microgreens require light to be grown, whereas sprouts are grown in darkness. In the case of sprouts, the entire plant is eaten, including the stem, the seed, and the root. However, with microgreens, the plant is trimmed from the base.

How Profitable Is the Microgreens Business?

In 2019, the microgreen industry was valued at over $1 billion, and it has been forecasted that by 2028, the industry will have grown to over $2 billion. More importantly, this is an industry with an incredibly high-profit margin. Regardless of the particular plant that you grow, you can expect to easily see a 50%-75% return on investment for each tray of microgreens that you produce. This can be pushed even higher if you sell at premium prices. The amount of money you make is entirely dependent on how much you sell. The more you grow, the cheaper it becomes to produce each tray.

How Much Investment Is Required?

One of the most attractive parts of this business is the low cost of entry. You can easily start a microgreens business with less than $100. Considering that you can make a make-shift solution for nearly all the material, the only real investment on your part will be to purchase the seeds. For less than $100, you can get a large number of different kinds of seeds and experiment with the process. Even if you plan to invest, you can set up a very good microgreen farming system complete with lighting, ventilation, and high-quality soil additives for your crop for under $1000.

What Is the Basic Equipment Needed?

The essential equipment in the microgreens business is the tray in which you plant the microgreens. Since they are so small, it can be a hassle to harvest them from the ground, which is why the preferred method is to plant them in trays. However, if you want to plant in the ground, this can be done too. If the natural conditions provide enough heat, light, and water, you won't have to invest in any of these accessories. Otherwise, the most common investments for microgreens farmers are getting better lighting and some sort of solution to provide ventilation and humidity management.

What Are the Necessary Skills?

There are no complicated sowing, growing, or harvesting techniques required for this business. The only thing you'll need is a little bit of patience, and not too much of that either. It is extremely easy to get started. The only learning curve is learning what your environment favors and how different plants behave in your local climate. However, given their small size, it is convenient to grow microgreens anywhere, and if it is not favorable outside, this can easily be done indoors.

What Is the Turnaround Time?

Another very attractive feature of this business is that the turnaround time is very short. In most cases, it can be a week, though, at a maximum, it will not exceed 21 days. Compared to any other kind of agriculture, this is a very small amount of time, and it also makes this business very profitable as within the span of a month, you can create multiple batches of microgreens.

What Is the Nutritional Value of Microgreens?

Microgreens of all kinds are extremely high in minerals, vitamins, antioxidants, and several beneficial components, so much so that they have been classified as being superfoods. Many microgreens are just as potent, if not more, than the fully developed versions of the vegetables that are derived from these plants. Moreover, they are plentiful in fiber which is also excellent for gut health. One of the most nutritious microgreens is red radishes.

Which Are the Easiest Microgreens to Grow?

The kind of microgreens that you'll be able to grow in your locality entirely depends on the weather and the growing conditions it provides. Some of the most resilient kinds of microgreens are cabbage, radish, cauliflower, and broccoli. These plants can withstand a variety of different conditions and are far less sensitive than varieties such as sunflower microgreens. However, more than the planting, it is the process that is challenging. But, once you are familiar with the germination process, it will be much easier from then on.

What Are the Most Common Microgreens?

Radish, cabbage, and other plants within the cabbage family are most commonly grown by microgreen farmers. There are some microgreens that are much higher profit items, and these are usually not as high selling, but because of the high profit that they create, they are preferred. Some other very common microgreens include varieties of herbs such as basil, cilantro, mint, and coriander. These are very highly demanded because of their aromas – and are often part of menus in upscale restaurants.

What Are Specialty Microgreens?

This includes things such as exotic varieties of beetroot, Chinese mahogany, and Shungiku microgreens. Specialty microgreens tend to vary a lot from region to region as there are certain plants that are not globally available. Moreover, some microgreens are farmed solely for their color and visual appeal, such as the exotic varieties of beetroot that are used just for their unique colors, whereas Shungiku is used for the distinctive design and style of the microgreen. If you are looking to create something unique, then look into what is commonly available in your area and work on that, or you can buy some specialty microgreens if you can find the seeds for them.

How Can I Research?

One of the most important things when gathering information for your business is to ensure that it is relevant and consistent with local trends. If you are relying on the Internet, then you are going to come across a lot of information that is really good, but it might not work in your region specifically because the available products are different and the customers that you are catering to are different. Ideally, you should look into official forms of research such as the statistics issued by the local Chamber of Commerce to gather information from resources with a more local perspective. Luckily, things don't change too much when it comes to microgreens, so insight that is a decade old will still be useful today.

How Do I Understand the Research?

The effectiveness of your research depends on how seamlessly you are able to integrate that into your business. Ideally, you should be looking for research that you can incorporate into the various business processes. Whether that is growing the plants or learning how to sell, you need a local perspective that can be an active part of your business.

How Much Time Is Required for Research?

Research can take a while. However, you shouldn't think of it as a chore that needs to be done. Rather, research is an ongoing process and something that you should be doing on a daily basis to improve your business. Even if you think you have understood everything there is to understand, continue researching to stay ahead of the curve because things are always on the move, and new equipment may be more effective.

How Much Money Is Required for Research?

Most of the best resources for research are completely free. However, if you want to learn from industry experts and talk to some of the greatest minds in the business, it could cost you quite a bit of money. That said, anything you invest in your education about the business will always be worth it in the long run.

How Can I Grow Microgreens Efficiently?

Growing the best microgreens is all about having a consistent environment and one that can facilitate your demand without taxing the plants. If you need 20 pounds of output, then invest in the solutions that will give you this result. When you are farming for yourself, you can withstand a few mistakes here and there, but for a business, a slight variation in the output could completely upset the profitability of that month and also cause problems in the supply chain.

What Are Some of the Microgreen Requirements?

Microgreens are very easy to manage if you know what they need. The main things to look out for are the condition of the soil, the temperature, the humidity, and the amount of water that the plants are getting. An excess or a lack of any of these components will lead to problems. Also, be sure to regularly change the soil or replenish it with the micronutrients that it needs.

How Can I Manage Infestations?

Different infestations and problems will arise due to different issues. There is no single thing that is always the cause of infestations. In many cases, it is due to too much water, but, in some cases, it could just be due to pests in the immediate environment. Since you're dealing with very small plants, there aren't any treatments that can be carried out, so your best bet is to keep the space extremely clean and physically try to protect the plants as much as you can.

How Do I Time Growing Microgreens?

The great thing about growing microgreens is that they have an incredibly fast turnaround time. In anywhere from 7 to 20 days, your product will go from seed to being ready to be sold. At the same time, this is also a bit of a challenge, as you need to time your growth in such a way that it meets customer needs. Microgreens can be stored, but they may not be the same after storage, and, ideally, you want to get the product fresh from the plant to the customer at the same time. It will help to forecast your sales and then plant accordingly. Even if you leave the plant in the soil for just a few extra days, it can cause them to overgrow and no longer be appropriate for your customers' needs. Understand the growth cycle of the plant you are growing and plan accordingly.

What Are the Business Licensing Requirements?

The other challenge with cutting microgreens and storing them is that it changes the legal requirements of your business. If you are growing and directly selling the product to customers, there isn't any licensing that you need to go through. However, if you are cutting the crop and storing it, then you need a proper business license, and there are a few other technicalities that you'll have to face. For instance, crops that are stored and then sold for human consumption need to be stored in a commercial refrigerator. This will increase the cost of business on your own, and the laws pertaining to refrigerated microgreens vary from state to state. So, if you are looking to sell across the nation, it can get complicated.

How Do I Register a Business?

As a small farmer, you can register yourself with the state or county, and you'll not have to worry about things such as compliance certifications and even tax returns. There is a minimum threshold that you have to meet in order to be liable to pay business fees, legal fees, and various forms of tax. When you are just starting out, this will not be a problem, but it is a good idea to have a look at your local legislation and find out how you can become a part of the legal business framework. You can quite easily do this yourself. However, there are a number of business consultants who can also help you with the process of business registration.

How Can I Reduce Costs?

One of the main expenses for people who are growing microgreens is the cost of electricity. The fluorescent lights, fans, and temperature control solutions can use a lot of power. To reduce your costs, you can consider investing in an outdoor setup, and if you want to get better control over the environment, you can also create a greenhouse. However, the most accurate and consistent results are achieved through artificial control of the environment. To make this a little more cost-effective, you can consider a solution such as solar power. This is a one-time investment and will reduce the costs significantly in the long run.

How Can I Get the Best Environment for Growth?

The largest microgreen farmers and the most profitable businesses often employ hydroponic solutions to grow their products. This reduces the cost to some extent and also gives you a lot more control over the entire process. Moreover, as this is done exclusively indoors, it protects you from all the various environmental changes and allows you to get a very homogenous product all year round, batch after batch. When you are growing outside, you have no control over things such as rain, snow, sunlight, and even the condition of the soil. It can be very time-consuming and cumbersome to manage all these variables, and it can end up costing more over the long run as compared to just investing once in a good hydroponics system. However, using hydroponics is a bit more technical.

How Do I Customize the Environment to Meet Plant Needs?

Ideally, you need to be able to have control over every factor concerning your plants to see what works best for you and how you can maximize the growth of the particular seed that you have. In some cases, you may find that what works for you is different from what works for other people and even from what the seed manufacturer recommends. The best modification you can make is to bring the plants indoors and use artificial lighting to control their growth. Along with this, improving the growing medium should also be a priority. These two things have a huge impact on the quality of the plants you produce and also influence your ability to consistently grow good microgreens on a continuous basis.

How Can I Find Clients?

Marketing is the best way to find clients. However, it's advised to get in contact directly with businesses as well, to find out whether or not they need your products. Institutions such as restaurants, wholesalers, and distributors will all be good options when you are reaching out to clients directly.

What Are the Costs of Advertising?

Online forms of advertising can be quite inexpensive, and some are even free. Traditional marketing is generally more expensive. However, even with digital marketing, it can be pricey when you are targeting a large audience, and you'll likely need to hire experts to optimize your marketing strategy to get the best results consistently and in the long term.

What Are the Best Business Management Solutions?

Technology is your best friend in the modern era if you are looking to grow your business. Everything from electronic plant management solutions to Customer Relationship Management (CRM) software to help manage the business will be helpful. The kind of solutions that you choose for your business depend entirely on the unique nature of your organization. As far as farming is concerned, it will be useful to employ some kind of technology to make the process more streamlined and help keep a better eye on things.

How Should I Scale?

Generally, businesses either tend to increase the sales volume or look to expand into more profitable niches. Most businesses use a combination of both these techniques to try and improve profitability. The path you choose will depend on what is feasible for you as a business and your market requirements.

How Do I Incorporate Microgreens into Diet?

Microgreens are best consumed raw. These vegetables are far too sensitive to be cooked or even steamed. You can use them to dress a salad, or you can simply add them to the food as a garnish.

Are Microgreens Affected by Seasons?

If you are growing your plants indoors, the only thing to consider is the temperature since they do have trouble growing in very cold or very hot climates. If you are growing outside, then keep an eye out for things like rain, snow, and various environmental conditions. However, it is relatively easy to provide microgreens with artificial forms of light. They are affected by seasons and environmental conditions, but you can easily control these variables.

Conclusion

Whenever you start a new project, whether that is a personal hobby or a business venture, it is a good idea to take a step back and look at the whole picture. While certain parts of the process may seem more attractive to you, and they may even be the main reason that you want to participate in something, you have to realize that you have to go through the entire process. This requirement of prioritizing the nitty-gritty aspects, as well as the areas you're fond of, can ruin the mood and make the activity seem not so enjoyable anymore.

Through the course of this book, we have provided a holistic idea of exactly what you need to do at every stage of the microgreen operation, both in terms of growing the microgreens to selling them, as well as giving readers some tips on how they can actually use the products that they are growing. Naturally, you may consider some aspects to be more interesting than others, or for some take precedence over others, but the reality is that every part of the process is equally important.

Also, you should keep in mind that business, farming, and every other activity under the sun requires time to perfect. Even the microgreens themselves require time to grow and reach maturity so if you are getting into this line of work, then be ready to put in some time. There are shortcuts to certain things, and it may be possible to speed up certain tasks. However, this is always at the cost of quality, whether that is the quality of the final product or the quality of how you do things.

The great thing is that if you take everything step by step – starting off from actually preparing the equipment you need through to selling the final product – you can do a very good job. In fact, you can do far better than you ever thought possible, given that you give the process the level of attention it deserves. At the end of the day, it boils down to how well you can internalize the information that has been covered and how effectively you can bring it to life. Just as microgreens need a certain amount of time to germinate and eventually grow, as a farmer and a business person, you'll also need some time to perfect the process. Don't be surprised if something goes wrong halfway through, or even if you don't launch in quite the way you had anticipated. The important thing is to learn from your mistakes and to keep growing, *both yourself and the plants.*

If you can perfect every part of the process and develop yourself to the extent where you can delegate these processes to a team, you can set it all on the right track and take a break. If you are looking to take this a step further than just growing microgreens for your own consumption, this is one of the best businesses to invest in and automate. It is very easy to maintain and *very profitable.* The deciding factor is how much effort you put into it.

Here's another book by Dion Rosser that you might like

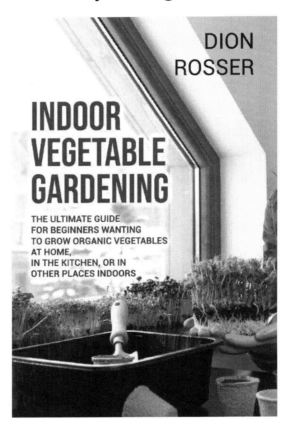

References

5 ways to eat microgreens. (2018, March 21). Back to the Roots Blog.

https://blog.backtotheroots.com/2018/03/21/5-ways-eat-microgreens

Apeace. (2014, May 6). What are microgreens, and why should you care? Urban Cultivator.

https://www.urbancultivator.net/microgreen

Apeace. (2015, June 12). Microgreens and sprouts are not the same things. Urban Cultivator.

https://www.urbancultivator.net/microgreens-vs-sprouts

EcoWatch. (2015, January 7). Why microgreens should be part of your daily superfood diet. EcoWatch.
https://www.ecowatch.com/why-microgreens-should-be-part-of-your-daily-superfood-diet-1881997999.html

Microgreens business... is it ACTUALLY PROFITABLE?? (n.d.). DonnyGreens. Retrieved from

https://donnygreens.com/blogs/microgreens-business/microgreens-business-is-it-actually-profitable

Microveggy. (2019, January 7). How to Eat Microgreens: 10 Healthy Ways to Enjoy their Green Power!

Microveggy.Com. https://microveggy.com/dish-recipe

etre, A., MS, & (nl), R. D. (2018, March 6). Microgreens: Health benefits, nutrition, and how to grow them.

Healthline. https://www.healthline.com/nutrition/microgreens

Saša. (2019, November 3). Are microgreens A good and profitable business? React Green.

https://reactgreens.com/are-microgreens-a-good-and-a-profitable-business

Sayner, A. (2019a, March 25). Complete a list of the main types of microgreens you can grow. GroCycle. https://grocycle.com/types-of-microgreens

Sayner, A. (2019b, April 16). Microgreens business: How to grow microgreens for profit. GroCycle.

https://grocycle.com/microgreens-for-profit

Wallin, C. (2019, January 18). How to start a microgreens business. Profitable Plants Digest.

https://www.profitableplantsdigest.com/how-to-start-a-microgreens-business

Ware, M., RDN, & L.D. (2019, November 7). Microgreens: Health benefits and growing tips. Medicalnewstoday.Com. https://www.medicalnewstoday.com/articles/316075

Warner, J. (2012, August 31). Tiny microgreens packed with nutrients. WebMD.

https://www.webmd.com/diet/news/20120831/tiny-microgreens-packed-nutrients

Miller, M. (2019, March 12). Is there any benefit to microgreens beyond looking adorbs? Women's Health. https://www.womenshealthmag.com/food/g26784840/what-are-microgreens

EspirituFounder, K. (2012, September 15). Building a microgreens business: Microgreens. Epic Gardening. https://www.epicgardening.com/building-a-microgreens-business-the-beginning

Jeena, L. (n.d.). How To Start A Microgreens Business – A detailed review. Gardening Heavn. Retrieved from https://gardeningheavn.com/microgreens-business

Microgreens growing equipment. (2020, June 16). Microgreens Entrepreneur. https://microgreensentrepreneur.com/microgreens-growing-equipment

Saša. (2020, May 26). 10 things you need to start growing microgreens like A professional. React Green. https://reactgreens.com/10-things-you-need-to-start-growing-microgreens-like-a-professional

Sayner, A. (2019, April 16). Microgreens business: How to grow microgreens for profit. GroCycle. https://grocycle.com/microgreens-for-profit

Wallin, C. (2019, January 18). How to start a microgreens business. Profitable Plants Digest. https://www.profitableplantsdigest.com/how-to-start-a-microgreens-business

87 types of Microgreens – the complete list of Microgreens for beginners. (2021, September 9). Microgreens Hub. https://microgreenshub.info/types-of-microgreens

BBC Gardeners' World Magazine. (2020, June 2). How to grow beetroot. BBC Gardeners' World Magazine; BBC Gardeners' World Magazine. https://www.gardenersworld.com/how-to-grow-plants/how-to-grow-beetroot

Chenell. (2021, July 17). 41+ fun types of microgreens to try growing. Seeds & Grain.

https://seedsandgrain.com/types-of-microgreens

Fanatic, R. G. (2020a, November 20). How to grow sunflower microgreens fast and easy. Epic Gardening. https://www.epicgardening.com/sunflower-microgreens

Fanatic, R. G. (2020b, December 11). How to grow broccoli microgreens fast and easy. Epic Gardening. https://www.epicgardening.com/broccoli-microgreens

Fanatic, R. G. (2020c, December 31). How to grow radish microgreens fast and easy. Epic Gardening. https://www.epicgardening.com/radish-microgreens

Fanatic, R. G. (2021a, February 19). How to grow corn microgreens fast and easy. Epic Gardening. https://www.epicgardening.com/corn-microgreens

Fanatic, R. G. (2021b, May 30). How to grow carrot microgreens fast and easy. Epic Gardening. https://www.epicgardening.com/carrot-microgreens

Fanatic, R. G., & NielsenEditor-In-Chief, L. (2021a, January 1). How to grow pea microgreens fast and easy. Epic Gardening. https://www.epicgardening.com/pea-microgreens

Fanatic, R. G., & NielsenEditor-In-Chief, L. (2021b, January 13). How to grow basil microgreens fast and easy. Epic Gardening. https://www.epicgardening.com/basil-microgreens

Fanatic, R. G., & NielsenEditor-In-Chief, L. (2021c, January 19). How to grow beet microgreens fast and easy. Epic Gardening. https://www.epicgardening.com/beet-microgreens

Fanatic, R. G., & NielsenEditor-In-Chief, L. (2022, January 18). How to grow cabbage microgreens fast and easy. Epic Gardening. https://www.epicgardening.com/cabbage-microgreens

Gazeley, H. (n.d.). How to grow cress for grown-ups. GrowVeg. Retrieved from

https://www.growveg.com/guides/how-to-grow-cress-for-grownups

How, G. K. (2015, May 6). How often should I water beets – learn how much water beets need. Gardening Know-How. https://www.gardeningknowhow.com/edible/vegetables/beets/watering-schedule-for-beets.htm

How to grow beetroot / RHS Gardening. (n.d.). Org.Uk. Retrieved from

https://www.rhs.org.uk/vegetables/beetroot/grow-your-own

Microveggy. (2018, September 20). Over 87 types of microgreens: Ultimate seed guide to growing your own.

Microveggy.Com. https://microveggy.com/types-of-microgreens

Radishes. (n.d.). Almanac.Com. Retrieved from https://www.almanac.com/plant/radishes

Sayner, A. (2019, March 25). Complete list of main types of microgreens you can grow. GroCycle. https://grocycle.com/types-of-microgreens

Soak And Soil. (2021, February 17). How to grow carrot microgreens (+benefits, FAQ, pests). Soak And Soil. https://soakandsoil.com/carrot-microgreens-how-to-grow-benefits-faq-pests

Types of microgreens. (n.d.). Hydrocentre Hydroponics. Retrieved from

https://www.hydrocentre.com.au/blog/types-of-microgreens

What are microgreens: Health benefits and growing tips. (n.d.). AllThatGrows. Retrieved from

https://www.allthatgrows.in/blogs/posts/nutritious-microgreens

(N.d.-a). Hgtv.Com. Retrieved from https://www.hgtv.com/outdoors/flowers-and-plants/vegetables/planting-and-growing-radishes

(N.d.-b). Hgtv.Com. Retrieved from

https://www.hgtv.com/outdoors/flowers-and-plants/flowers/growing-sunflowers-when-to-plant-and-how-to-grow-sunflowers

Facebook users by country 2021. (n.d.). Statista. Retrieved from https://www.statista.com/statistics/268136/top-15-countries-based-on-number-of-facebook-users

Khan, T. N. (2020, January 17). [start-it-up] how to start microgreen farming business? Entrepreneur Europe. https://www.entrepreneur.com/article/345171

Sayner, A. (2019, April 16). Microgreens business: How to grow microgreens for profit. GroCycle.

https://grocycle.com/microgreens-for-profit

Gibson, A. (2013, March 10). Easy guide to growing microgreens. The Micro Gardener.

https://themicrogardener.com/easy-guide-to-growing-microgreens

Hill, F. (2013). How to grow microgreens: Quick, easy ways to grow and eat nature's tasty superfoods. Frances Lincoln.

Moran, N. (2017, November 29). Managing diseases in microgreens. Produce Grower.

https://www.producegrower.com/article/managing-diseases-in-microgreens

Sayner, A. (2019, April 16). Microgreens business: How to grow microgreens for profit. GroCycle.

https://grocycle.com/microgreens-for-profit

Microveggy. (2018, December 8). Growing microgreens outdoor vs. indoor. Retrieved from Microveggy.com

website: https://microveggy.com/outdoor-vs-indoor

Smith, J. (2021, August 1). Growing microgreens indoor vs. Outdoor. Retrieved from Types Of Microgreens

website: https://typesofmicrogreens.com/growing-microgreens-indoor-vs-outdoor

Victory, D. (2021, March 23). How to grow microgreens outdoors. Retrieved from VictoryGarden.blog website: https://victorygarden.blog/grow-microgreens-outdoors

Vanderlinden, C. (n.d.). How to grow your microgreens. Retrieved from The Spruce website:

https://www.thespruce.com/grow-your-own-microgreens-2540008

Pepin, P., Eve, & greenadmin. (2019, April 18). Best tips for selling microgreens. Micro Greens Farmer.

https://microgreensfarmer.com/where-to-sell-product-from-your-microgreens-business/

Where to sell microgreens: 5 best places. (2021, May 1). RusticWise.

https://rusticwise.com/where-to-sell-microgreens

Apeace. (2017, August 2). 8 microgreen dishes to celebrate the best of summer. Urban Cultivator.

https://www.urbancultivator.net/summer-microgreen-recipes

Hamama. (n.d.-a). Blackened shrimp guac cucumber bites with garlic greens. Hamama. Retrieved from https://www.hamama.com/blogs/recipes/blackened-shrimp-guac-cucumber-bites-with-garlic-greens

Hamama. (n.d.-b). Garlicky chive micro-herbs Chutney with Naan Bread. Hamama. Retrieved from

https://www.hamama.com/blogs/recipes/garlic-chive-chutney-with-naan-bread

Hamama. (n.d.-c). Garlicky chives micro-herbs pull-apart bread. Hamama. Retrieved from

https://www.hamama.com/blogs/recipes/garlic-chive-pull-apart-bread

Hamama. (n.d.-d). Roasted potatoes with browned butter, sage & garlicky chives micro-herbs. Hamama. Retrieved from https://www.hamama.com/blogs/recipes/sage-butter-potatoes-with-garlic-chives

Hamama. (n.d.-e). Walnut garlic greens pesto. Hamama. Retrieved from

https://www.hamama.com/blogs/recipes/walnut-garlic-greens-pesto

How to Make Microgreen Salads – a recipe for filling in seasonal eating gaps. (2020, March 2). Rootsy Network. https://rootsy.org/microgreen-salads

Microgreens roasted Squash balsamic vinaigrette salad dressing recipe. (n.d.). Yummly.Com. Retrieved from https://www.yummly.com/recipe/Microgreens-Roasted-Squash-Balsamic-Vinaigrette-Salad-Dressing-1505939

Pineapple orange, green smoothie with Microgreens recipe. (n.d.). Yummly.Com. Retrieved from https://www.yummly.com/recipe/Pineapple-Orange-Green-Smoothie-with-Microgreens-9407262

Made in the USA
Coppell, TX
16 January 2023

11179033R00085